IN THE IMAGE OF GOD

A BIBLICAL VIEW OF HUMANITY

WILLIAM H. BAKER

MOODY PRESS

CHICAGO

© 1991 by
THE MOODY BIBLE INSTITUTE
OF CHICAGO

All Scripture quotations, unless noted otherwise, are from the *Holy Bible: New International Version.* Copyright © 1973, 1978, 1984, International Bible Society. Used by permission of Zondervan Bible Publishers.

ISBN: 0-8024-4125-4

1 2 3 4 5 6 7 8 Printing/VP/Year 96 95 94 93 92 91

Printed in the United States of America

IN THE
IMAGE
OF GOD

Contents

Preface

Judging from its perceived needs and ways of attempting to meet those needs, one of humankind's greatest areas of ignorance is biblical truth about itself. I suspect that this is more a matter of neglect of the Bible than repudiation of the Bible. The sciences of anthropology and psychology are the two most prominent attempts to understand humanity, but they seem to proceed more in independence of biblical teaching than in refutation of it; the Bible is simply ignored.

There is much even in biblical theology that is built upon the nature and condition of the human race. For example, the fact of human depravity and the extent of it largely determines the whole structure of the doctrine of salvation. The doctrine of eschatology, or study of last things, is essentially the outcome of human depravity. The doctrine of sanctification, the process of becoming holy, rests on the strange phenomenon of indwelling sin in the Christian and the need to reduce it.

Two tendencies are prevalent when people think about themselves. Either they think too highly of themselves or they think too little of themselves. The first tendency leads to selfishness, oppression, and even war, whereas the second leads to depression and emotional imbalance. Biblical anthropology provides an antidote to these tendencies. It cautions us against pride in its doctrine of depravity, and it offers a basis for affirming our worth in its doctrine of the image of God.

Most of the works on biblical anthropology are written for advanced theological students. This book is designed for the average layman or college student and is written in simple language with theological terms explained and nothing taken for granted so far as the reader is concerned. It is my conviction that the average person needs desperately to understand himself, perhaps even before he pursues other biblical teachings to any extent. Hopefully this volume will make a contribution to this need.

1

HUMANITY'S ORIGIN

The Bible tells how humanity came into existence. Other ancient accounts and mythologies do the same thing, but the biblical account is notably different in several ways.

First, the biblical account is free from fantasy. The Babylonian myth of Marduk[1] teaches that he killed the dragon Tiamat and created heaven and earth from the two halves of its body. The Bible is sublime by comparison.

Second, the biblical story of creation is free from contradictions to scientific fact, although some modern *theories* of science seem to contradict it. Adam is created from the "dust of the ground," an ancient expression that can be understood, without symbolizing it, as the basic elements scientists now realize compose the human body. Many in the ancient world believed in a three-storied universe, but Genesis has no such reference (if properly translated) in light of post-Copernican astronomy.

Third, the biblical creation story accords with common sense and the universal observation that all effects have an adequate cause. Humanity's unique and complex existence as personality is best explained as having been caused by a greater personality, such as the God of the Bible. Modern materialistic evolution teaches, on the other hand, that all life emerged from inanimate, nonpersonal material, a contradiction of all scientific, empirical observation of the universe. This is not substantially better than ancient myths that taught that finite, bizarre creatures or human-like gods brought man into existence.

THE HISTORICAL REALITY OF ADAM AND EVE

Were Adam and Eve actual people who lived in time and space on this planet? This belief is widely denied by classical liberals, and the answer will have profound effects on how we understand humanity's original condition as well the way we interpret certain other parts of the New Testament. There are three major views concerning the reality of Adam and Eve: the traditional, or orthodox, view espoused by fundamentalists and some evangelicals; the neoorthodox view, which is also held in part by many evangelicals; and the classical liberal view.

THE TRADITIONAL, OR ORTHODOX, VIEW

The traditional view takes the Bible in its literal, or normal, sense and assumes that Adam and Eve were actual historical people. Adherents contend that there is no obvious reason that Scripture intends the names of Adam and Eve to be "generic" names for "mankind." Hebrew names are usually given to reflect character or the aspirations of the parent for the child. Thus, it might not be unusual that God gave the first human the name "Adam," which means "man," because in many ways he would typify subsequent human beings.

THE NEOORTHODOX VIEW

Emil Brunner is primarily responsible for the view that the modern theory of evolution, if taken seriously, forces us to take Adam and Eve as divinely inspired legends or symbols that stand for every one of us.[2] In other words, each of us experiences a temptation and fall at some point in his life. The strength of the view is that it makes each one responsible for his own sin and avoids the difficult idea that Adam acted in our behalf, making us all sinners by representation—a conclusion reached by many evangelical interpreters of Romans 5:12.

THE CLASSICAL LIBERAL VIEW

A commentary on Genesis written during the early part of the twentieth century typifies the classical liberal view of Adam and Eve.[3] According to the author, John Skinner, Genesis 1-3 is a legend of some religious value (a "myth" would have little or no religious value, like the Babylonian creation stories) but of no scientific credibility. The Genesis story presents the facts that God is one and humanity was originated by Him, and that is essentially all it does religiously. Liberals do not believe that God is trying to say anything about humanity in Genesis but that humanity is trying to say something about God. Parts of the Bible may contain truth about God, but the story of origins has limited value. We must depend wholly on modern science for knowledge of human origins. Neither has humanity "fallen" from anything but is rather climbing away from its animal ancestry.

CONCLUSION

Although the neoorthodox view takes the creation and fall of Genesis seriously as a true theological statement, though not historical, it faces the same problem of · the classical liberal view in that it must ignore that the apostle Paul seems to consider Adam and Eve real historical individuals in Romans 5 and 1 Corinthians 15. Thus, to deny the historicity of Adam and Eve is to deny the full inspiration of these important statements about the origin of sin.

The liberal view, of course, totally discounts the biblical record of origins and views it as having little or no theological value. If one wishes to regard the biblical narratives as reliable records, the traditional, orthodox view is the only tenable position.

THE BIBLICAL CREATION ACCOUNT

THE GENESIS ACCOUNTS

Man, the pinnacle of creation (Gen. 1:26-31). The description of humanity's creation as part of the six days of creation comes as a climax to everything else. First, there was the creation of light (Gen. 1:3), then the dividing of water from water vapor (Gen. 1:7), then the emergence of dry ground (Gen. 1:9), and next vegetation (Gen. 1:11). Then the sun and moon appear (Gen. 1:14), followed by the creation of living sea and animal life (Gen. 1:21, 24), and finally Adam (Gen. 1:26). Each, in its turn, was declared "good" (Gen. 1:10, 12, 18, 21, 25), but following Adam's creation, the term "very good" is used (Gen. 1:31). Without Adam the creation was not complete, so far as God was concerned. The Hebrew word "good" (*tob*) means "excellent" and stands in contrast to what resulted later from sin.[4]

Humanity is related to God in a special way, for it is created in God's "image" and "likeness" (Gen. 1:26). This places humanity in a superior position to the rest of animal life, and its meaning will be explored in chapter 2. This "image" evidently gives humanity the capacity to rule over all other animal life. Both male and female possess this image (Gen. 1:27), suggesting that man and woman are equals intellectually and spiritually.

Humanity's supremacy includes dominion over animal and plant life (Gen. 1:28-30), and God commanded Adam to "increase in number" and "subdue" the earth (Gen. 1:28). Recently, humanity's abuse of its environment has been erroneously traced to this command, as though subduing the earth means flagrant and destructive dissipation of its resources.[5] What it really means is that we should utilize the earth and its resources for our true good and God's glory. Conservation is a part of this. Our pollution of the environment arises out of the evil passions of our corrupted nature, not God's mandate.

Humanity, a material masterpiece (Gen. 2:7). The second account of creation is typical of ancient Near Eastern literature where such a recapitulation adds further details to the first story (not evidence of another ancient document blended together with the first as some critics allege).[6] God "forms" Adam from "the dust of the ground." The picture is of a potter and his clay, a somewhat different idea than the word "create" of Genesis 1:27 (see Jer. 18:6 for a use of the same word "form"). The stress is on the creative artistry of God and gives a hint of the beautiful organism called the human body. Into this masterpiece God breathes the "breath of life," a life shared with all the animals (see Gen. 1:30).

Humanity, intellectual beings (Gen. 2:19-20). The fact that Adam and Eve were made in God's image implies that they were rational, or intellectual, beings, but further evidence for this is found when Adam gives names to the animals, a form of identification. This is an activity requiring a measure of knowledge and logical ability. Genesis makes no reference to Adam's going through a process of education, however, unless his creation implies an accelerated learning process. At any rate, humanity has had knowledge from the very beginning.

Humanity, both male and female (Gen. 2:20-25). By causing the animals to pass before Adam (2:20), God apparently impressed Adam with the immense gap that existed between himself and the beast. None was a "suitable helper" for him. Presumably, such "suitable helpers" had been created for each species of animal: a female counterpart for the purpose of reproduction. Eve was created to fill that function, but she became more than a mere sex partner. Several facts bear this out: (1) She is uniquely formed out of a part ("rib"—the Hebrew is somewhat vague) of Adam, implying that the man without the woman is incomplete;[7] (2) she is a "suitable helper," and this means literally "helper of his kind," which implies equality to Adam;[8] thus, she is Adam's intellectual complement; (3) she is one to whom her husband becomes "united"—a blending and absolute commitment of two personalities —as well as "one flesh," which according to 1 Corinthians 6:16 appears to be *sexual* union.

Last of all, Genesis 2:25 suggests that, prior to the occasion of the first sin, there was an absence of "shame" between the man and the woman, so far as the physical relation was concerned. This could be called "moral innocence," and its precise meaning may be a mystery to us until the effects of the Fall are entirely removed. But since final redemption takes humanity far beyond mere innocence and makes it fully righteous—unable to sin—we may never know what this meant.

Humanity's value (Gen. 9:6). To say that humanity is created in the image of God implies great value, simply by that expression alone (see chapter 2). Genesis 9:6, however, puts the expression "image of God" in juxtaposition with the shedding of blood—premeditated, malicious murder —and thereby creates a unique way to measure the value of a human being: "Whoever sheds the blood of man, by man shall his blood be shed; for in the image of God has God made man."[9]

According to much modern social morality and judicial thinking, capital punishment is a flagrant *disregard* of the value of human life, as though the act of murder and the act of society's taking the life of the murderer are the same species of crime. But Genesis 9:6 says that just the opposite is true: punishing a murderer by taking his life *declares* the value of human life, and in this case nothing else is of greater value than what God created in His own image.

OTHER BIBLICAL ACCOUNTS

Genesis is the prime source for information about humanity's origin, but several other biblical passages further clarify the creation narratives of Genesis.

HUMANITY'S DIGNITY (PS. 8:4-8)

Although humanity is insignificant in comparison to the vast universe (Ps. 8:3-4), nevertheless God has set tiny humanity over the creation. (See Ps. 8:5-6, where the psalmist contemplates humanity's great dignity, if not its immensity.) Value and importance are not necessarily commensurate with size or extent ("great things come in small packages").

The phrase "You made him a little lower than the heavenly beings" (cf. "angels" of Heb. 2:7, which is quoted from the Greek Septuagint) is puzzling, because the word translated "heavenly beings" is the Hebrew *elohim*, which can mean "God" in some contexts and "angelic beings" in others.[10] If this means "heavenly beings" it pertains mostly to humanity's rank among God's creatures. If it means "God" it refers to the image of God in humanity and points to dignity. Humanity's position is so great that David sees it as a cause for praise and gratitude (Ps. 8:9).

HUMANITY'S ORIGINAL UPRIGHTNESS (ECCLES. 7:29)

Solomon searched for an upright man and found only one among a thousand (Eccles. 7:28).[11] He explains this situation as fully humanity's fault, not God's: "God made mankind upright, but men have gone in search of many schemes." This accords with what we learned from Genesis 3:1-6 and with Paul's statement in Romans 5:12, that sin "entered the world through one man," not through God. God created man capable of sin, but God did not cause sin or create man a sinner.

Both the words "very good" in Genesis 1:31 and "upright" in Ecclesiastes 7:29 need to be clarified morally. Was Adam morally and spiritually righteous in an absolute or a qualified sense? If it was absolute righteousness, how then did he commit the first sin? Chapters 2 and 3 will further discuss this problem.

HUMANITY, MORAL BEINGS (ROM. 9:21)

Paul, like Jeremiah (18:1-6), uses the analogy of the potter and the clay to make his point that God is the sovereign Creator. The context of Romans 9 is a discussion of those on whom God has mercy and those He "hardens." Because God has made people the way they are, Paul senses that his readers might infer from his words that people really have no moral responsibility. Paul rebukes this belligerent attitude in verse 20, and his words about God's right to deal with His creatures as He pleases must mean that He deals with them according to their moral acts. God has every right to do this, even to the extent of bearing with them patiently when they happen to be "objects of his wrath" (v. 22).

Thus, the teaching of this passage is just the opposite of what many have supposed it to be: that God makes "objects of his wrath" on one hand and "objects of his mercy" on the other (vv. 22-23). If one takes a closer look at the precise meaning of the words, he will actually find support for the moral responsibility of humans. In these descriptions God "endures" the objects of His wrath with "patience," which suggests that God does not cause their sin. Furthermore, these "objects" are "prepared for destruction," a word that emphasizes *process*[12] and that also lacks the word "beforehand," pointing to a preparation during their lifetime. The objects of mercy, on the other hand, are "prepared in advance," a word that means "*appointed* [by God], probably in eternity past, another way of speaking of divine election."[13] People are the instigators of their own sin, not God, whereas God is the instigator of people's salvation. People are moral, responsible beings.

WOMAN: CREATED FOR MAN'S SAKE (1 COR. 11:9; 1 TIM. 2:13)

Paul teaches that the Genesis record of human creation in which Adam was first created and then Eve was formed from his body to be his "helper" implies that the man had authority over the woman as her "head" (1 Cor. 11:3, 8-10), and she should not be his authoritative teacher in the church (1 Tim. 2:11-12). The precise nature of the meaning of the word "head" is in debate among Christians today, but I prefer the view that "authority over" is the meaning of the word "head" in 1 Corinthians 11 as well as in 1 Timothy 2:11-12.[14]

CONCLUSION

The biblical description of the creation gives us the distinct impression that human beings have great dignity and worth. Moreover, they are creatures capable of genuine moral decisions who, at a point, made the decision to go contrary to God's specific command. Adam and Eve were not created as sinners but *became* sinners. God made them with no moral flaw to occupy a position of great prestige and rank over the creation, second only to angels in the heavenly realm. They were specially related to God through the "image of God" in which they were created.

THE EVOLUTIONARY VIEW OF HUMAN ORIGIN

The view of human origin that dominates the scientific world today is biological evolution. Several varieties of evolution exist. *Atheistic evolution* is the view that God does not exist and that the Bible is essentially mythological; humans, by natural processes alone, evolved from lower forms of life to their present state. Life is the product of the right combination of elements and billions of years of random selection. Humanity will ultimately rise above this animal ancestry and cease to do evil, provided it does not destroy itself in the meantime. But given enough time, it will reach moral perfection. This view dominates science fiction as well as the New Age movement.

Many Christians, however, hold to evolution as a process, while not necessarily subscribing to the idea of moral evolution. They believe in the existence of God and in the full reliability of the Bible as well as in the theory of evolution, with some qualifications. Adherents of this view, since they also accept the Bible as the Word of God, do not oppose any of the theological or moral truths concerning humanity that we have already discussed.

EVANGELICAL VIEWS THAT SUBSCRIBE TO SOME FORM OF EVOLUTION

In some sense God is involved in the evolutionary process according to Christians who believe in an evolutionary theory. There are several variations within this school of thought, but they all have in common several things: (1) belief in the work of God in creative evolution; (2) the interpretation of the "days" of Genesis 1 as "ages," not twenty-four hour days (a legitimate understanding in some uses of the word "day"),[15] which enables them to accept the great amount of geological time required for evolution; and (3) a general tendency to identify Genesis 1-11 as a "poetic" genre of ancient literature, thus not to be interpreted literally throughout.[16]

Theistic evolution. Some Christians[17] accept a rather conventional form of evolution in which Adam is the first true human in the chain of evolution. Into a highly evolved creature God placed His image, and this is what scientists would call *homo sapiens*. Adherents of theistic evolution want to do justice to the Bible, but the theory involves several hermeneutical (interpretive) problems.

The first of these is that the Bible says that human-kind was made from the "dust" of the ground. If this is not taken literally it would have to be regarded as a poetic myth or a reference to Adam's evolutionary ancestry. But the phrase "for dust you are, and to dust you will return" (Gen. 3:19) seems to make an evolutionary ancestry unlike-ly. Second, theistic evolution has difficulty accounting for the teaching that woman was made from Adam, not from "dust."

Progressive creation. Progressive creation takes the view that God immediately created the major "species" and then allowed them to evolve (known as "micro evolu-tion").[18] Thus, evolution of an animal ancestry to humans or evolution of one species to another ("macro evolution") is rejected. This conforms more to the Genesis description of life-forms being created "after their kind."

This view has much to commend it, but it must con-front the following criticisms: (1) the creative day-ages do not conform very well to the actual geologic ages, i.e., the biblical order of life-forms does not coincide with geo-logy;[19] (2) the expression "evening and morning" must be taken in some nonliteral way.

ATTEMPTS TO DEAL WITH THE PROBLEM OF SIX DAYS

The linguistic problem of interpreting the expressions "evening and morning" and "day" has been solved in other ways by those who are inclined to be more literal in their interpretation and yet subscribe to some form of evolution. They have produced two different approaches.[20]

The revelatory day view. The "revelatory day" theory of Genesis 1 sees the creation days as literal but as references to days during which God *revealed* the successive stages of creation to Moses, not days during which anything was ac-tually created. Scripture, of course, gives no clue that this is the way the days are to be understood.

The six initial days of creation theory. The "initial day" view proposes that the reference to six days as well as the expression "evening and morning" is to the *first day* of each geologic age. During each of these initial twenty-four-hour days the process of micro-evolution was begun with all the necessary mechanisms of evolution being provided within a literal twenty-four-hour span of time. A geologic age then followed in which the evolutionary process took place. Though this theory tries to take the days literally, there is no biblical basis for assuming indefinite periods between the twenty-four-hour days.

SOME NONEVOLUTIONARY PROPOSALS

THE "GAP" THEORY

Some Christians, while not impressed by the claims of evolution, nevertheless are convinced of the great age of the earth implied by uniformitarian geological science (if processes of the past took as much time as they do today—i.e., are "uniform" with current processes—then the earth must be billions of years old). Thus, adherents of the "gap" theory believe that an accounting must be made for this vast amount of time and that the Bible must provide some clue to it.[21]

The "gap" theory is an effort to remove the disparity between the biblical account of creation in six days and the scientific evidence for the great age of the earth by placing a gap of time between the original creation of Genesis 1:1 ("in the beginning God created the heavens and the earth") and the six days of creation beginning with Genesis 1:3 ("Then God said," and so on). Such a "gap" is implied, they maintain, in the language of Genesis 1:2: "And the earth was formless and void, and darkness was over the surface of the deep." One form of this theory hinges on the translation of "the earth was formless and empty" into "the earth *became* formless and empty," which they believe is implied in the Hebrew verb "was." In addition, they cite Isaiah 45:18, which says that the earth was not created as a formless and empty waste, thus it must have become that way later.

Yet another variation of the gap theory[22] places the gap *prior* to Genesis 1:1, making the original creation before that verse in time. Thus, Genesis merely tells the story of re-creation; one would have to go to such passages as Isaiah 45:18 or Hebrews 11:1 for biblical descriptions of the "original" creation. This version of the gap theory avoids the linguistic problem of translating the Hebrew "was" as "became."

In either case, the gap provides time for a pre-Adamic, catastrophic judgment that wiped away that original creation. Adherents of the gap theory also postulate that the judgment of Satan and his evil angels took place during this time and probably actually caused the judgment of a race of pre-Adamic humans now extinct, thus explaining the fossil record of geology and anthropology. (For Satan's judgment, see Isa. 14:12-14; Ezek. 28:13, 15-17; Rev. 12:4).

Criticisms of the gap theory are as follows: (1) Romans 5:12 teaches that sin entered the world through Adam. Is this to be restricted to the "second" creation, or is it absolute, so that death never existed before Adam? If the latter is meant, then Romans 5:12 precludes the gap theory, because the gap theory theorizes that death existed before Adam; (2) few Hebrew scholars would translate "the earth *became* formless and empty";[23] (3) the words "formless and empty" elsewhere mean "barren," and this might easily mean "without the order and life that is to follow."

SCIENTIFIC CREATIONISM (FIAT CREATION)

A growing minority of Christian scientists[24] believes that there is an absolutely scientific way to explain origins that also allows for a normal, literal interpretation of the Genesis creation account. Such an approach, naturally, would appeal to those with a more literal approach to the Bible.

First of all, they are convinced that evolution is an inadequate model by which to explain origins and processes; even some noncreationist scientists have been calling attention for a long time to some deficiencies in evolutionary theory as scientific knowledge has increased. For example, evolution appears to contradict the second law of thermodynamics, which implies that the universe is "winding down" not evolving, going toward greater disorder, not greater order as evolution assumes. Another example is in the paleontological record of fossil humans, which seems to *assume* what it is proving in its reconstruction of the evolutionary history of humanity with great imagination. Many of those fossils may even be mere apes, the scientific creationist argues. Evolutionists, of course, have their answers to these objections.[25] They would argue that the second law of thermodynamics operates as such only in a "closed system," and the earth may not be a closed system. As to the criticisms of the fossil reconstruction of humanity, they would argue that creationists simply do not take the evidence seriously and flippantly dismiss it.

Another contention of the scientific creationist is that the phenomenon of the earth's crust as given by uniformitarian geologists can be better explained by a relatively recent creation of six days and rearrangement of the earth's surface by the catastrophic flood of Noah's day. Such "flood geology," or "catastrophism," assumes a universal flood based on the language of Genesis 7:11-23, where the waters covered the highest mountains and wiped out all life on earth.

Finally, the scientific creationist admits that the Bible was not intended to be a scientific textbook in the strict sense, but since the Creator inspired it, it can provide valuable insights for the scientist's own pursuit of knowledge. Because of this assumption, such things as a six-day creation, an actual universal flood, and a relatively young earth constitute its basic premises.

THE AGE OF HUMANITY

How long ago did God create Adam? The answer depends on one's view of origins. Any form of evolution, including progressive creationism, is deliberately formulated to allow for the evidence, especially from geology, for an immense amount of time for humanity's physical or intellectual development. Scientific creationism with its "young earth" theory, taking the Bible as its starting point, is a startling contrast to this.

Evolutionary anthropologists differ as to when humans reached the point where they were truly *homo sapiens*. Some believe it was when they learned to make tools, from 500,000 to 2 million years ago.[26] Others believe it was when humans began to bury their dead, about 50,000 years ago.[27] If language is his distinguishing characteristic, humanity is 30,000 to 40,000 years old.[28] This latter view is preferred by most progressive creationists, because the biblical record describes Adam and Eve as able to speak. However, the Bible describes Adam's immediate descendant, Cain, as practicing agriculture, and this was not developed, according to anthropologists, until the Neolithic period, 20,000 years later. There are suggested solutions to this, but the whole question of humanity's age is at this time a matter of debate among those who accept the findings, generally, of evolutionary anthropology.[29]

The scientific creationist, of course, considers the date of creation *and* Adam to be virtually the same because of his literal view of the six days of creation. Therefore, he would place the creation of humanity in light of the biblical geneologies (with reasonable accounting for gaps between some names) as somewhere between 4000 B.C. to 10,000 B.C.[30]

A Perspective on Human Origins

With genuine, godly Christians disagreeing on the subject of the precise nature of human origins, what is an open-minded Bible believer who may not be a scientist to conclude?

First of all, we should bear in mind that everyone is in substantial agreement about the basic biblical facts concerning human creation. In other words, whether he believes in some form of evolution or not, every Christian who believes the Bible is in some sense a "creationist." Unlike his nontheistic counterpart in the scientific community, he assumes the existence of the biblical God who created heaven and earth.

Second, one's belief in the exact nature of human origins, so long as he believes that God was in the beginning, does not necessarily have any bearing on his relationship with God. Christians today face dangers to their spiritual welfare, but mere evolutionary theory as a theory of human development is not one of them. True, humanistic evolution—where a person is totally sufficient apart from any God—can devastate society, and many are unwittingly falling prey to this.

Third, so far as the Bible student is concerned, the fundamental issue is hermeneutics. But even if one, for example, believes that Genesis 1-11 is largely poetic, he nevertheless regards it as *divinely inspired* poetry and thus takes it seriously as a statement of basic theological truths —truths such as the divine creation of humanity, its fall into sin, and divine providence. He does not consider it to be poetic without basing it on what he considers to be a good reason, such as the name of Adam being symbolic of "man."

Fourth, it is hazardous and presumptuous to assume that those who take a certain position on creation/evolution are necessarily motivated by some unworthy influence. Creationists are often accused of taking their position out of disregard for the scientific evidence and of being dominated by traditionalism and fundamentalism. On the other hand, theistic evolutionists are accused of caving in to establishment science out of a desire to be accepted by other scientists. I believe it is possible for a person to believe what he does because he sincerely thinks the evidence is on his side when it comes to this particular issue; I know and respect many who disagree with my own position.

I prefer scientific creationism. But I readily acknowledge that my preference is due more to hermeneutical reasons than to the weight of scientific evidence. Perhaps if I were a scientist I might be more influenced by scientific evidence that supports an evolutionary conclusion, though my reading of the scientific evidence pointing to a creationist view gives me a certain amount of confidence in its intellectual respectability.

The hermeneutical reasons for my preference are as follows: (1) the lack of grammatical and stylistic reasons for regarding Genesis 1-11 as poetic and nonliteral; (2) the lack of contextual reasons for interpreting "day" as an age rather than a twenty-four-hour period; (3) the unconvincing attempts to make sense out of the Hebrew expression "evening and morning" as anything other than a reference to a calendar day; (4) the linguistic evidence that the Flood was universal and the consequent explanation it provides for the geological evidence; (5) the widely accepted hermeneutical principle that a word or phrase should be taken literally if it makes sense and figuratively if the literal makes no sense.

Regarding this last hermeneutical principle, I am inclined to interpret in a way that would have made sense to the author and his original readers, which is what I mean by "literal." If a respected scientist can provide an interpretation of the scientific data that enables me to do this, I prefer to go with him.

Nevertheless, we should realize that at this point in our understanding of science and the Bible we would be unwise to "buy in" to any view as we do certain other biblical teachings. We should be open to any theory that can do a better job of reconciling science with the Bible.

THE ORIGIN OF THE SOUL

The Genesis account of humanity's creation makes clear that Adam and Eve were created as beings with both a material and immaterial part. The immaterial part is often referred to as the "soul," and the creation account uses the terms "living soul" and "image of God." Just what these are composed of is the subject of the next chapter.

The question here is: What is the origin of the soul? One response might be that it was created when Adam was formed and God put the breath of life into him. The problem with that answer is that perhaps only Adam's and Eve's souls were created at that time, and other souls are created when people are either conceived or born. Souls, after all, are individual and personal.

One early Father of the church, Origen, believed that the soul preexisted before time began.[31] According to him, the soul was created eternally, and its present state is only one epoch in its existence. Since there is no biblical support for such a theory, we will look at two points of view that have more biblical evidence.

CREATIANISM (OR CREATIONISM)

The creatianist view (not to be confused with the Genesis creation) is that the soul is created immediately or directly by God and placed into the body either at conception or at birth or at some time between. Advocates believe it explains the unique individuality of the child apart from what it inherits from its parents. Some creatianists believe that this pertains to the "spirit," not the "soul"; they believe that the soul is transmitted by parents, whereas the spirit, which is humanity's highest part, is directly created at conception or birth. This view has been held by most Roman Catholics[32] and Reformed theologians.[33]

The objection to the creatianist view is that it appears to make God the creator of moral evil, and this seems to contradict the biblical teaching that man was created without sin, as we have already noted. One way to avoid this is to teach that people *become* sinners rather than have a disposition toward sin from birth, but this conflicts with such passages as Psalm 51:5 and Ephesians 2:1, which imply that a person is a sinner from conception. The other alternative is to hold that the soul is created pure and placed into a body that will inevitably corrupt it. Some would respond to this solution by explaining that God is still indirectly responsible, because no human choice is involved in such corruption; in this scheme corruption is unavoidable. In this view, the "sin nature" is distinct from the soul and transmitted, along with the body, by one's parents.

TRADUCIANISM

Tertullian, an early church Father, first taught the view that God created all souls, or perhaps all the "material" for souls, when He created Adam.[34] In modern times Reformed theologians William G. T. Shedd[35] and Augustus Strong[36] have preferred it. According to the Traducian view the soul and the body are transmitted from Adam through one's parents (hence the word "traducianism" from the Latin *traducere*, "to transfer"). This view denies that there is any separate existence or consciousness of a soul before conception. God, of course, because He is omniscient, knows who everyone will be from eternity. Though there is no direct biblical evidence for this view, the following deductions are reasonable: (1) God seems to have created humanity as a species with Adam (Gen. 1:27) and "breathed" into him the breath of life only once (Gen. 2:7); (2) Adam fathered a son in his own "likeness" (Gen. 5:3), which suggests a transmitted soul; (3) God "rested" (ceased) from His creative work on the seventh day, which implies that all creative activity may have been complete by the sixth day; (4) Romans 5:12 teaches that all humanity sinned "in Adam," and traducianism would best fit this with its seminal idea of all souls being created in Adam and thus in some sense "participants" with Adam in his sin; (5) Hebrews 7:9-10 implies that people are in some sense participants in the deeds of their ancestors: "One might even say that Levi, who collects the tenth, paid the tenth through Abraham, because when Melchizedek met Abraham, Levi was still in the body of his ancestor."

CONCLUSION

The question of the origin of the soul is a matter of marginal importance. However, what one believes should be consistent with what Scripture teaches, and in this case the concept of the human race's guilt in Adam—a far more crucial doctrine—could be at stake. Looking at an issue from every angle often leads to sounder conclusions. Consequently, the Traducian view seems to make the most sense biblically.

FOR FURTHER THOUGHT

1. Why is belief in God as Creator superior to atheistic evolution?

2. Why does the idea of Adam's creation in the "image of God" give humankind greater dignity?

3. Basing your answer solely on the biblical creation account, debate the two statements that follow:
   a. God created male and female in His own image, thus God Himself is *both* male and female; thus male and female are equal.
   b. God created male and female in His own image, thus both possess the image of God and are equal.

4. Discuss the merits and demerits of these two statements:
   a. Capital punishment *denies* the value of human life.
   b. Capital punishment *enhances* the value of human life.

5. Discuss the following assertion: Evolution and creationism should be given equal attention in public schools. (Limit the debate to the question of what constitutes a good education, not the question of religion in public schools.)

6. Why is scientific creationism in such disrepute among most scientists?

FOR FURTHER READING

Harris, Laird. *Man—God's Eternal Creation*, pp. 7-71. Chicago: Moody, 1971.

Lammerts, Walter. *Scientific Studies in Special Creation*. Grand Rapids: Baker, 1971.

Mixter, Russell L., ed. *Evolution and Christian Thought*. Grand Rapids: Eerdmans, 1959.

Morris, Henry. *The Troubled Waters of Evolution.* 2d ed. El Cajon, Calif.: Master, 1975.

Pun, Pattle P. T. "Evolution." In *Evangelical Dictionary of Theology*, edited by Walter A. Elwell, pp. 388-92. Grand Rapids: Baker, 1984.

Strong, Augustus H. *Systematic Theology*. Philadelphia: Judson, 1907: pp. 465-95.

NOTES FOR CHAPTER 1

1. Enuma Elish, Tablet IV. *The Babylonian Genesis*, ed. and trans. Alexander Heidel (Chicago: U. of Chicago, 1951).

2. Emil Brunner, *Man in Revolt* (Philadelphia: Westminster, 1948), pp. 85-88.

3. John Skinner, *A Critical and Exegetical Commentary on Genesis*, International Critical Commentary (New York: Charles Scribner's, 1910), pp. 4-12.

4. Francis Brown, S. R. Driver, and Charles Briggs, *A Hebrew and English Lexicon of the Old Testament* (Oxford: Oxford U., 1978), p. 374. W. S. LaSor, David A. Hubbard, and Frederic W. Bush (*Old Testament Survey* [Grand Rapids: Eerdmans, 1982], p. 74) reflect the common evangelical interpretation, namely, that the purpose of the several references to "good" (Gen. 1:4, 10, 12, 18, 21, 25) is to build a contrast to the story of the Fall in Genesis 3 (i.e., that God started everything without sin, but sin entered through Adam).

5. Lynn White, Jr., "The Historical Roots of Our Ecologic Crisis," *Science*, March 10, 1967; cited by Francis A. Schaeffer in *Pollution and the Death of Man: The Christian View of Ecology* (Wheaton, Ill.: Tyndale, 1970).

6. See Gleason Archer, *A Survey of Old Testament Introduction* (Chicago: Moody, 1964), pp. 117-24, for a good summary of this phenomenon in ancient Near Eastern literature.

7. Since later in the New Testament the single state is recommended for those so "gifted" (1 Cor. 7:25-38), I am inclined to think that a man can be "complete" with the help and friendship of women without necessarily being married. So also for women. This passage, therefore, is not a statement that everyone should be married. Men need women and vice versa *apart* from the marriage union.

8. Thus C. F. Keil and Franz Delitzsch, *The Pentateuch*, Biblical Commentary on the Old Testament (Grand Rapids: Eerdmans, n.d.), 1:86. E. A. Speiser (*Genesis*, The Anchor Bible [Garden City: Doubleday, 1964]), in loc., calls it literally "alongside him" or "corresponding to him."

9. For a further development of the idea that the "image of God" implies humanity's value, see William Baker, *On Capital Punishment* (Chicago: Moody, 1985), pp. 103-5.

10. Peter C. Craigie (*Psalms 1-50*, Word Biblical Commentary [Waco, Tex.: Word, 1983], p. 108) gives a good summary of the interpretation of this phrase. He opts for the translation "a little lower than God."

11. Ecclesiastes reflects the limited observation of a man "under the sun" (see Eccles. 1:14). Thus, we must be cautious in making Solomon's observation concerning women a biblical or divine absolute (Eccles. 7:28b). Solomon does not appear to have been attracted, as a rule, to women of spiritual quality, especially later in life (see 1 Kings 11:1-6) and thus might easily say what he does here out of igno-

rance. The book of Ecclesiastes must be interpreted with care. It is inspired in the sense that it faithfully reports human wisdom, often unaided by divine revelation, and numerous internal remarks make this clear.

12. William Arndt and F. W. Gingrich, *Greek-English Lexicon of the New Testament and Other Early Christian Literature*, 2d ed. (Chicago: U. of Chicago, 1979), p. 417.

13. Ibid., p. 705.

14. In classical literature "head" (Gk. *kephale*) on some rare occasions means "source" and on other rare occasions means "authority over." The question of which of these Paul intends in these passages concerning women is a matter of controversy among evangelicals, especially in the debate over the role of women in the church and in the home. If the Septuagint version of the Old Testament influenced Paul, the meaning "authority over" might be valid. Feminist writers consider the Septuagint to be irrelevant and stress the influence the classical usage of "source" when Paul metaphorically uses the word "head." For the viewpoint that "head" means "source," see Berkeley and Alvera Mickelsen, "What Does Kephale Mean in the New Testament?" in *Women, Authority and the Bible*, ed. Alvera Michelsen (Downers Grove, Ill.: InterVarsity, 1986), pp. 97-132. For the opposing viewpoint that "head" means "authority over," see Wayne Grudem, "Appendix 1," in George W. Knight, *The Role Relationship Between Men and Women in the Church* (Chicago: Moody, 1985).

15. The Hebrew lexicon of Brown, Driver, and Briggs lists the use of *yom* with "evening and morning" (Gen. 1:5; and elsewhere) separately in the category of a twenty-four-hour period of time (p. 398). Nonliteral uses are represented by "day of the Lord" (Amos 5:18) and "harvest time" (Prov. 25:13), this latter use coming the closest to "age."

16. LaSor, Hubbard, and Bush (*Old Testament Survey*, p. 74) are typical of this approach: "It conveys theological truths about events, portrayed in a largely symbolic, pictorial literary genre."

17. See Richard Bube, *The Human Quest* (Waco, Tex.: Word, 1971), for a development of theistic evolution by a Christian.

18. See Pattle P. T. Pun, *Evolution: Nature and Scripture in Conflict?* (Grand Rapids: Zondervan, 1982), for a development of progressive creationism.

19. See Henry M. Morris, *Biblical Cosmology and Modern Science* (Nutley, N.J.: Craig, 1970), pp. 56-71, for a thorough discussion of the lack of correspondence between geologic ages and the order of creation in Genesis 1.

20. See D. England, *A Christian View of Origins* (Grand Rapids: Baker, 1972), for a brief development of these views with objections to them.

21. See G. H. Pember, *Earth's Earliest Ages* (Grand Rapids: Kregel, 1975), for full development of the gap theory.

22. Merrill F. Unger, *Commentary on the Old Testament* (Chicago: Moody, 1981), 1:5.

23. Harold Stigers (*A Commentary of Genesis* [Grand Rapids: Zondervan, 1976], p. 49) speaks directly to this syntactical issue: "The construction of 'became void,' etc., is not justified by Hebrew syntax. When the verb 'to be' (*hayah*), is to be construed as 'became,' the addition of the prepositional *lamedh* is required with the following word to provide this meaning, and this preposition is absent here." Examples of this are in Genesis 2:10; 48:19; and Exodus 4:3.

24. See Henry M. Morris and Duane T. Gish, *The Battle for Creation* (San Diego: Creation Life Publishers, 1976).

25. See Pun, *Evolution*, for answers to the creationist arguments.

26. Donald R. Wilson, "How Early Is Man?" *Christianity Today*, Sept. 14, 1962, pp. 27-28.

27. Paul H. Seeley, "Adam and Anthropology: A Proposed Solution," *Journal of the American Scientific Affiliation* 22 (Sept. 1970): 89.

28. James W. Murk, "Evidence for a Late Pleistocene Creation of Man," *Journal of the American Scientific Affiliation* 17 (June 1965): 37-49.

29. See Millard Erickson, *Christian Theology* (Grand Rapids: Baker, 1986), p. 485, who prefers it because it has the fewest difficulties. He lists the various attempts to solve this problem (pp. 486-87) but admits that there is insufficient data for any final conclusion.

30. Henry Morris, *Biblical Cosmology*, pp. 56-71.

31. Origen, "Origin De Principiis," 11:9:6, in *The Writings of Origen*, trans. Frederick Crombie (Edinburgh: T. and T. Clark, 1895), 1:132-33.

32. George D. Smith, ed., *The Teaching of the Catholic Church* (New York: Macmillan, 1958), 1:211-12.

33. Charles Hodge, *Systematic Theology* (Grand Rapids: Eerdmans, 1940), 2:70-71.

34. Tertullian, "On the Soul," chaps. 26-27, in *The Fathers of the Church: Apologetical Works*, trans. Edwin A. Quain (New York: Fathers of the Church, Inc., 1959), pp. 240-45. Quain says, "Tertullian's doctrine of Traducianism is implicit in his discussion of the origin of the body and soul. Just as the body was generated from the body of the parents, so the soul of the child is derived from the soul of the father and mother at the moment of conception" (p. 243, n. 1).

35. William G. T. Shedd, *Dogmatic Theology* (reprint; Grand Rapids: Zondervan, n.d.), 3:249-60.

36. Augustus H. Strong, *Systematic Theology* (Philadelphia: Judson, 1907), p. 494.

2

THE IMAGE OF GOD

Humanity is a unique creation. Scientists may explain this uniqueness in terms of man's ability to reason, but even that has to be the result of evolution. In such a scheme of things humankind is still regarded as essentially an animal, though an intellectually superior one.

The Bible, however, teaches that humanity's uniqueness resides in its being created in the image of God. This image probably includes the intellect, but it is much more. Apart from the Bible there really is no adequate basis for peoples' thinking of themselves as unique. It is significant that the Judeo-Christian tradition, rooted in the Scriptures, has been the primary influence in the world to maintain the value and dignity of human beings. Respect for life is one of the cornerstones of Judaism and Christianity.

The complete phrase in Genesis 1:26 is "in our image, according to our likeness." The relation between *image* and *likeness* has puzzled readers and scholars for centuries. Usually the two words are synonyms in the Old Testament.[1] Thus, there is ordinarily no distinction between them. But in the grammatical construction here, each one may carry a distinctive emphasis. Hebrew scholars have suggested that the root meanings may provide a clue. The root meaning of "image" (Heb. *tselem*), though not certain,[2] may be "to carve" or "to cut,"[3] as of carving a likeness of something, and thus may mean in Genesis 1 that Adam is a representation of God. The word for "likeness" (Heb. *demuth*) is more clear in its root meaning: "to be like."[4] Together the phrases may mean that Adam is a representation of God who is like God in certain respects.[5]

VIEWS OF WHAT THE IMAGE CONSISTS

Broadly speaking, the idea of the image of God means that humanity has a unique relation to God. There is something about God that is also true of human beings but is not true of animals. It is what gives humanity special dignity, significance, and value. Christians have offered various suggestions as to precisely what the image consists of. It can be categorized as an inner quality (held by most orthodox theologians since Augustine), as a relationship between God and humanity (held by neoorthodox theologians such as Karl Barth and Emil Brunner), as dominion over nature (held by some recent theologians such as Leonard Verduin), as a representation of God (held by evangelical theologian G. C. Berkouwer), or as sonship (suggested by H. D. McDonald).

THE IMAGE AS AN INNER QUALITY

The view that identifies the image as an internal quality, such as psychological make-up, reason, some spiritual quality, personality, or moral awareness has prevailed for most of Christian history.[6] Some would include the Mormon idea of God's having a body in this category, but such a view is foreign to the biblical teaching of the spiritual nature of God.

The "inner quality" must correspond, of course, to something about God Himself that is not found in animals and that makes human beings distinctive. In fact, it is such an image that makes the incarnation of Christ possible and makes Christ in His humanity the perfect example of what the image is.

THE IMAGE AS A GOD–HUMAN RELATIONSHIP

The relationship view identifies the image as humanity's relation to God, at its strongest when faith is present, according to Emil Brunner.[7] This image was brought about when God produced in humanity the freedom, responsibility, and answerability that He wished. An analogy of this can be seen as someone stands before a mirror and perceives both an intangible personality (or "spiritual" reality) as well as a physical being. This view includes both the immaterial and material being of humanity, but it does not imply that God Himself has a material part.

The point of the analogy is not in the similarity between the subject (God) and His reflection, but in what the subject wants the mirror to reflect. For example, if a flashlight is reflected in the mirror, the reflection is what is intended, but if the mirror is turned around so that it no longer reflects the light, the reflection is hampered even though the light is still there. In the same way, sin hampers our relationship to God, like the turning of the mirror, even though man never ceases to have the image in him. Faith is like turning the mirror straight again so that everything is reflected as God intended. Karl Barth extended the idea of the relational image to relationships between humans, a kind of "partnership" or *ability* to relate.[8] In fact, the image is centered in the fact that humanity was created both male and female, two people who were related to each other.

THE IMAGE OF DOMINION

Leonard Verduin proposes a view of the image of God that identifies the image as something a person *does*.[9] In Genesis 1:27-28, Adam, who has just been described as having been created in God's image, is commanded to exercise dominion over the earth. This phrase is taken, therefore, to be the definition of the image. Humanity is different from the animal and plant realms in its lordship over all creation.

THE IMAGE AS REPRESENTATIVE OF GOD

The representational view is proposed by theologian G. C. Berkouwer and is quite similar to the inner quality view but adds a few unique twists.[10] Humanity, according to his view, is intended in its whole being to represent God primarily as a holy being. The Old Testament commands people to be "holy" (Lev. 11:45-46), and Jesus said, "Be perfect as your heavenly Father is perfect" (Matt. 5:48). Furthermore, the apostle Paul taught that the regenerated "new self"—the believer—is being "renewed in knowledge in the image of its Creator" (Col. 3:10). This line of teaching looks to Jesus Christ for its best definition of that image, since He is the very image of God (Col. 1:15).

THE IMAGE AS SONSHIP

H. D. McDonald believes that all the ideas included in the views just described could be combined into the idea that sonship was the purpose for which God created humanity and that this constitutes the image.[11] To support this, McDonald lists the following kinds of evidence: Luke 3:38 calls Adam the "son of God"; Jesus Christ is the image of God because He is uniquely the Son of God; and believers are the image of God by the way "image," "glory," and "sonship" are used. Thus, believers are carrying out the mandate to express in themselves the image of God.

CONCLUSION

Since the thing that makes humanity truly unique and different from the animal realm—and Genesis 1 and 2 seem to be stressing this point—is its spiritual, rational, and moral capability, the view that equates the image of God with the inner quality of humanity is most likely.

As to the dominion view, the biblical reference to humanity's dominion is probably less of a definition and more a statement of what *results* from humanity's having a spiritual, rational, and moral capacity. In other words, it is the presence of the image of God in people that makes them *able* to exercise dominion over the earth. Dominion itself is not what constitutes the image.

So far as the relationship view is concerned, although it is ingenious, the relationship between humanity and God is *possible* because of humanity's unique moral and intellectual capacities. Relationship is not by itself significant but is a *result* of intrinsic qualities that God placed within human beings. True, God wanted a creature with whom He could relate in a special way, but in order to do this, He had to bring into being a particular kind of being, one made "in His image."

The view that humanity is a representative of God seems to be a blending of features of the inner quality view and the relational view. Like the relational view, Jesus Christ is the model, and to some extent this is valid, short of the fact that for Jesus Christ to be the "image of God" includes full deity. Certainly we can learn from Jesus' perfect humanity what ours is going to be some day. But the same weakness in the relational view is true also of the view that humanity represents God. God desires that a person be a representation of Himself, but to do that He must create a kind of being with the capacity to do so, and that brings us back to the idea of a quality within humanity that constitutes the image, the inner quality view.

The sonship view seems similar to both the relational and representational views. Sonship is a rich and complex relationship with God, and when it is functioning as it should it is a representational thing as well. But it suffers from the same criticisms: it is because of an intrinsic quality in a person that he is *able* to be a son. Besides this, it is difficult to see unregenerate humans as having the image if believers are sons in the sense of the image of God, for believers *become* sons by adoption. When McDonald says that Christ is the image of God because of His unique sonship, I question the theological soundness of his argument. It is the incarnation that makes Jesus the image of God to humanity, and this is something quite different from the image that we are attempting to define.

The Original Form of the Image

What was humanity's moral condition when God first created it? One might think it sufficient to say simply that it was without sin. A deeper probing of exactly what this means has been a pastime among theologians for centuries. The serpent implies in Genesis 3:5 that in some sense Adam and Eve might not know "good and evil" until they eat of the tree of "the knowledge of good and evil." Someone has quipped that they already knew good by virtue of their being in the Garden and by knowing God, and all that Satan was really offering was the knowledge of evil, which is not much of a bargain.

THE REFORMED VIEW

Several answers to humanity's moral condition before the Fall are available. Louis Berkhof[12] and Augustus Strong[13] describe Adam and Eve before the Fall as in a state of moral perfection, righteous or holy, and that this is part of the image of God. However, they were able to sin, and this is not a part of the image of God. More recently, Anthony Hoekema has qualified this as a conditional state in which humanity was not yet a "finished product." Humans needed to grow and be tested. They were "able not to sin" but "not unable to sin."[14]

The Bible uses the words "righteous" and "holy" in both the absolute sense when they are applied to God and the relative sense when they are applied to human beings. It is "relative" in the sense that no human is absolutely sinless, but by faith he can be declared righteous and, as a whole, can be characterized as righteous. God is righteous in that He *cannot* sin, but Adam and Eve certainly were able to sin, and believers (saints) certainly are able to sin. Because of these qualifications, it perhaps is not accurate to use the word "righteous" of humanity before the Fall.

THE ROMAN CATHOLIC VIEW

Roman Catholics prefer the description "perfect innocence," in which humanity was devoid of positive righteousness. They also believe that there was a natural tendency, because of humanity's "lower appetites," to rebel against the higher powers of reason and conscience.[15] This "concupiscence," as it is called, was not itself sin but merely the occasion for sin. The problem with this idea is that "lower appetites" comes close to being "an inclination toward sin," and this is really not perfection of any sort; in fact, it seems to be a result of the Fall: an inclination toward evil. You can understand why they postulate this "natural tendency" to rebel against humanity's "higher powers," because they are trying to explain where sin came from, and it is hard to do this if Adam was perfect.

THE ARMINIAN VIEW

The Arminian view is similar to the Calvinist or Reformed view in that the words "righteous" and "holy" are used of Adam before the Fall, but it is different in that Adam and Eve are also referred to as "innocent," meaning that they had free will to do either good or evil.[16] Arminius even went so far as to say that Adam and Eve had an inclination to good by virtue of the properties of the image of God in them.[17]

CONCLUSION

The best way to clarify the idea that humanity was without sin by creation is to say that it was "innocent" but not necessarily with any disposition to do good. Perhaps the best word to clarify the situation is "neutral." To say that Adam and Eve were "holy" or "righteous" might imply to some that they had a disposition to obey God, and without a sin nature it becomes difficult to explain why they sinned. God, I believe, was not directly responsible for their sin except that He planned that they should be *able* to sin by His eternal decree, which means that their sin was certain to occur yet not caused by Him, since God in His foreknowledge knows what will actually happen, given certain circumstances.

To summarize, the following comparison may be helpful: (1) Adam was morally *neutral* by creation; (2) fallen humanity has a disposition *against* God; (3) regenerated humanity has a disposition *in favor* of God; (4) glorified humanity will be *confirmed* in its disposition *in favor* of God.

VIEWS OF HUMANITY'S COMPONENT PARTS

Certain texts of the Bible seem to describe humanity as though it consists of certain basic parts. For example, 1 Thessalonians 5:23 says, "May the God of peace himself sanctify you entirely and may your spirit and soul and body be preserved complete without blame at the coming of our Lord Jesus Christ." In this text, two words, "spirit" and "soul," describe something invisible, whereas "body," of course, refers to that part of humanity that is visible. Can people be divided into distinct parts? Are some of these parts more important than others? In other words, what is the basic constitution of human beings?

THE TRICHOTOMIST VIEW

The trichotomist believes that human beings are composed of three distinguishable parts: body, soul, and spirit. The word "trichotomy" is Greek for "cut into three parts." This idea was held by the early church Father Irenaeus[18] and in more recent times by the great German scholar of the nineteenth century, Franz Delitzsch.[19] The widely used *Scofield Reference Bible* teaches it in its notes, thus passing it on to a large segment of evangelical Christians.[20]

Some consider that unregenerate humanity has lost the component called "spirit" (which they relate to the "likeness" of Genesis 1) while retaining a "soul" (which they relate to "image"). This sharply distinguishes between two words that are basically synonymous in Scripture.

The trichotomist view is based primarily on such passages as 1 Thessalonians 5:23, in which Paul the apostle prays that God will keep blameless the "whole spirit, soul and body" until Jesus comes. Also important to the proof for this view is Hebrews 4:12, which seems to teach that the soul and the spirit can be "divided" by the sword of the Word of God, hence making them separate entites.

THE DICHOTOMIST VIEW

The dichotomist (from the Greek, "cut into two parts") believes that humanity is composed of two principal parts: body and soul (or spirit). His line of proof generally amounts to a refutation of the proofs the trichotomist uses and in some cases a philosophical assumption that everything is composed of either physical or immaterial reality. The dichotomist view has probably been the most widely held throughout history, and such eminent theologians as Louis Berkhof,[21] Augustus Strong,[22] and Gordon Clark[23] have preferred the view.

Examples of the dichotomist's arguments are that 1 Thessalonians 5:23 is no more a statement of humanity's only principal parts than the words of Deuteronomy 6:5, which commands us to love God with all our heart, soul, and strength (to which Jesus added even a fourth—mind —in Mark 12:30). Rather, 1 Thessalonians 5:23 is one of several ways to describe the whole being by combining three of the many *aspects* of this being.

So far as Hebrews 4:12 is concerned, the dichotomist calls attention to the grammatical point that the preposition "to" in the phrase "it penetrates even to dividing soul and spirit" actually means "up to the point of division" but not actual division. Last of all, he calls attention to the fact that the words *soul* and *spirit* are used interchangeably throughout the Bible and at most are merely aspects of the same essential thing, humanity's immaterial being.

In recent times, some liberal theologians have developed a variation of dichotomy better described as "dualism."[24] Such a sharp distinction is made between body and soul that the New Testament concept of resurrection is rejected in favor of the immortality of the soul alone. Dualism, therefore, is essentially a system that places more value on the soul in the belief that physical things are of much less consequence, and it is repugnant to them to think of the body as having eternal significance.

MONISM, OR RADICAL UNITY

If dichotomists tend to attack trichotomy as their primary form of defense of their view, neoorthodox theologians who believe in monism are largely reacting against dichotomy.[25] They dislike the idea of a separation between the physical and the spiritual and prefer instead the idea that a person is a radical unity: "self." To be human is to have a body, not merely a soul or mind.

The monistic idea is a reaction against the old liberal idea of the immortality and primary value of the soul. Its adherents believe that their view is supported by the fact that there is no Hebrew word for "body" (Gk. *soma*). The closest word in Hebrew is *basar*, but this means "flesh" and is more often translated by the Greek word *sarx*, which means "flesh." The New Testament references must be understood in light of this Hebrew concept of the body and soul being a radical unity, not in the traditional way, which argues a sharp distinction between them.

ESSENTIAL UNITY

Theologian Millard Erickson[26] proposed a view that he calls "conditional unity," a view of humanity's constitutional nature that he believes is more biblical and philosophically acceptable. He rejects trichotomy for reasons similar to those of the dichotomist (see above). He is not satisfied with traditional dichotomy, seeing some validity in the monist's objections to it from the Bible and philosophy and thus seeks for an alternative. He also has difficulties with the monistic view because of the biblical teaching of the intermediate state, in which it appears that humanity is actually separated from the body between death and resurrection in a disembodied, spirit state.

Human beings are a unity, Erickson declares, and this is the physical-spiritual condition in which they were created. But in 2 Corinthians 5:6-8 Paul teaches that the believer can be "away from the body and at home with the Lord" (v. 9), a condition which he prefers (v. 8) to the groaning and burden of being in the body (v. 4). But Paul longs to "be clothed" with the "heavenly dwelling," or new resurrection body. Thus, the intermediate state is an incomplete, temporary condition to be preferred over humanity's present condition of physical decline, pain, and suffering, but second in preference to the restored creation condition of body-spirit. The truth in monism must be brought into greater harmony with the biblical teaching.

According to conditional unity, then, the biblical terms "soul," "spirit," "heart," "mind," "body," and "flesh" are references to one's self, or humanity, aspects of a unified being that God ideally always intends to exist as such, except during the eschatological period of the intermediate state. It is this view that seems best to fit the biblical data.

THE QUESTION OF HUMANITY'S FREEDOM OF CHOICE

Is humanity, which is created in the image of God, free to make choices by virtue of special endowment by God? This question has been answered in the affirmative as well as in the negative.

THREE BASIC VIEWS

Whatever one's belief in God, he or she can be categorized in one of three ways regarding human freedom: determinism, indeterminism, and self-determinism.

Determinism. "Determinism" can be either naturalistic or theistic. Naturalistic determinists, such as the psychiatrist B. F. Skinner, believe that environment and heredity are determining causes for all human decisions and acts. To put it another way, for everything that happens there are conditions that make that act the only thing that could have happened. Theistic determinists, such as Martin Luther and Jonathan Edwards, believe that instead of impersonal conditions for causes it is God who predetermines or foreordains all things (more on this later).

To those who oppose determinism of either kind, such an idea fails to allow sufficiently for the human personality and its ability to cause acts, but, worse than that, it does not explain a person's responsibility for his actions. Indeed, the famous trial lawyer Clarence Darrow was noted for defending clients on grounds that they were mere victims of circumstances, and this theory has apparently influenced modern justice to a large degree.

One determinist, John Feinberg, defends his view of determinism by what he calls "soft determinism" or "compatibilism."[27] By this he means that there are "nonconstraining sufficient conditions" for human decisions. People act according to their desires (thus they are free), but those desires can be influenced through reason.

That raises the question of what influences a person to sin, since Feinberg believes that God has predetermined *all* things, even evil and sin. Feinberg's answer is that God does not tempt anyone to evil (James 1:13-15), that sin stems from the creature and God cannot be implicated in sin. He makes no attempt to discuss the immediate influence of sin, but presumably he would attribute that to Satan.

Indeterminism. "Indeterminists" can also be classified into naturalistic and theistic schools of thought. Naturalistic indeterminist William James believed that human acts are totally uncaused, that any human act could have been otherwise.

Theistic indeterminists, of course, introduce God into the picture and such indeterminists as James Arminius believed that God limited His sovereignty to the extent that human beings are totally free (more on this later).

Indeterminists do believe that the will can be influenced but that an act is "free" if it is not causally determined; that is, no cause is *sufficient* to determine one choice or another.

Self-determination. Some theists are self-determinists, something of a middle ground between determinism and indeterminism that arises out of their interpretation of Scripture. Such famous Christians as Thomas Aquinas and C. S. Lewis fell into this category. This view is that a person's acts are caused by himself. There are factors such as heredity and environment that can influence behavior, but they are not determinative. It may be that inanimate objects need outside causes, but personal beings created in the image of God can actually exercise free will. One can believe in self-determination and still accept the concept of God's predetermining of all things, as in the case of the theistic determinist.

Some would object that this implies there really is no cause for a human decision, that nothing causes the will to decide. The answer might be that *persons* are the cause, that people make decisions *by means of* the will. They are created in God's image, which means they have free will.

Others would object that such a view is incompatible with the biblical doctrine of predestination. Part of the answer would be that the Bible teaches *both* the ideas of free will (Matt. 23:37; John 7:17; Rom. 7:18; 1 Cor. 9:17; and 1 Pet. 5:2) and predestination (Eph. 1:11; Rom. 8:28-30) and that there is an unexplainable mystery or paradox that must simply be accepted.

THE QUESTION OF PREDESTINATION

The theistic versions of all the views discussed above accept, since God is sovereign in some sense, some form of divine predestination. The relation between sovereignty and free will varies in each of the views. Basically, however, there are two fundamental concepts of divine sovereignty: specific sovereignty (Calvinistic) and general sovereignty (Arminian).

Specific sovereignty. The strictest form of specific sovereignty is that God is the ultimate cause of all things, including sin. Nevertheless, God holds human beings accountable for everything they do, and this must simply be accepted because God will be glorified through it all—this is the ultimate matter of importance.

A somewhat moderate form of specific sovereignty is that God "decrees" all things, and thus all things are certain to occur as they do. This decree allows for the possibility of evil, because God decreed that humans should have free choice. Thus, some kind of qualification enters the eternal decree of God in which God is described as *permitting* evil in order to allow for true human freedom, or a distinction is made between the *certainty* of all things to occur and the *causing* of all things to occur as they do. In either case, since humans do what they desire, they are free and responsible creatures. If God permits evil, He is not responsible for it; if He causes evil, He is responsible.

General sovereignty. General sovereignty means that to the extent that God gives people freedom, He does not control earthly affairs. But God does have the ability within this scheme to accomplish "general" goals (hence "general sovereignty"). Such general goals would be the death of Christ for sin, the general progress of history and movement of nations, and the ultimate triumph of good over evil. Such goals would require limited divine influence and intervention.

This would explain how biblical predictions can be made and how prayer could be answered. God, who is omniscient, knows what people will do in the future. One form of general sovereignty is that God has actually limited what He knows about the future. He has not predetermined the future, except to the extent that He does work for general goals. When someone prays, the future is actually changed by God by limited intervention of some sort.[28]

Such a view, its proponents insist, is the only viable way to explain why God can *desire* everyone to be saved in spite of the fact that not everyone *will* be saved. Those who take the previous view that God knows what all people will do, hold that God foreknew who would believe, then predestined those particular people to do just that, thus making it truly their choice, not God's. Those who believe that God has limited his knowledge of who would believe, believe that He cannot possibly have been the cause of their belief or unbelief.

One problem with general sovereignty is whether God can logically guarantee that anything is certain in His general plan when, in reality, so many human decisions are involved in everything that happens. To guarantee the outcome of anything, would God not have to exert overpowering influence or intervene in such a way as to coerce many decisions such that they would not really be free?

Another obvious problem with general sovereignty is the existence of scriptural passages that seem to teach that God predestines all things (Eph. 1:11). A frequent answer to this is that free will was foreordained, and in that sense alone God predestined all things. In the case of God's self-limitation of His knowledge, there is simply no explicit reference in the Bible of such limitation by God; in fact, there is much to imply that God indeed knows all things, including all future things (Isa. 46:9-10).

THE BEARING OF THE FALL ON HUMAN FREEDOM

The freedom Adam and Eve had at creation is not exactly the freedom we have now. We will discuss the total effect of the Fall upon the image of God in the next chapter, therefore just a few comments will be necessary here about human will.[29]

Humanity was created with the capacity for choice. Morally speaking, Adam and Eve were, according to Augustine, "able not to sin," the biblical way to describe "true freedom." The ability to sin would not be called "freedom" by the Bible, but instead "bondage." This condition prevailed until Adam gave in to the temptation to eat of the forbidden fruit. When that occurred, this ability not to sin was lost, and humanity became "not able not to sin" (John 3:34; Rom. 6:6, 17, 20).

Upon faith and regeneration, humanity's true freedom is restored, so that people are again "able not to sin" (Gal. 5:1, 16). They continue to be plagued by sin, but if they yield to the Holy Spirit, they are "able not to sin."

Someday, when believers receive their new, glorified bodies, sin will be fully eradicated, and regenerated people will realize their true freedom perfected. When this happens they, like Jesus, will be "not able to sin" (1 Cor. 15:42-44; Rev. 21:4; 22:3).

CONCLUSION

The time has come to reach a conclusion regarding the matters of determinism and God's sovereignty. The view of human freedom that seems most in accord with Scripture is that which involves a combination of self-determination and specific sovereignty. Self-determination seems best to allow for the dignity of humankind created in the image of God, and the concept of specific sovereignty does the most justice to the character of God as revealed in Scripture as well as such specific passages as Ephesians 1:11. If sovereignty means that God has made all things certain to occur as they actually do in history but does not imply constraints on the will at the time decisions are made, people can still be regarded as fully responsible beings (also the clear teaching of Scripture) whereas God is in ultimate control and can predict the future. Prayer is meaningful simply because God has chosen to act in response to prayer, which He Himself has "induced" but not constrained.

In the final analysis, there are things that are not explainable to our finite minds. Full rationalization of this conclusion above is not possible. Whatever our position, we must allow for *both* the sovereignty of God and the responsibility of humanity. People must never be reduced to robots, and God must never be reduced to a finite being —even if by His own choice. Anything else simply will not accord with the biblical material.

A WORD TO THE CHRISTIAN: THE POWER OF THE HOLY SPIRIT

For the believer, at least, one concluding thing needs to be stated. Believers have a freedom not enjoyed by the unbeliever. That freedom is to recognize their helplessness to do God's will independently and consciously to surrender themselves to the empowering of the Holy Spirit as they decide to obey God (Gal. 5:16-17). The ability to make decisions to obey God lies within the believer, but the carrying out of those decisions is not within his power.

Furthermore, even the decision to obey God is one that is influenced in some way by God Himself. On one hand, we are commanded to "work out" our salvation—to carry out its implications of obedience (Phil. 3:12)—but at the same time God is at work in us, influencing us to decide to obey and then giving us the ability to obey (Phil. 3:13).

FOR FURTHER THOUGHT

1. What is different about the biblical view of humanity's present condition in relation to the views we are taught in secular schools?

2. What is different about the biblical view of humanity's creation in the image of God insofar as what we are taught in secular schools?

3. Why is it important to realize that humanity was originally without sin, that God did not create people as sinful beings?

4. Why is it important to reject the idea that only a person's soul has ultimate value?

5. If one accepts the concept of the unity of humanity, why is the resurrection so significant?

6. To what extent is the concept of humanity's dignity and uniqueness threatened by the concept of naturalistic determinism?

For Further Reading

Barth, Karl. *Church Dogmatics*, 3:1, 183-214. Edinburgh: T. and T. Clark, 1956-60. (Neoorthodox)

Berkouwer, G. C. *Man: The Image of God*, pp. 67-118. Grand Rapids: Eerdmans, 1962. (Modern Reformed Evangelical)

Brunner, Emil. *Man in Revolt*, pp. 91-167. Philadelphia: Westminster, 1948. (Neoorthodox)

Erickson, Millard J. *Christian Theology*, pp. 495-517. Grand Rapids: Baker, 1986. (Evangelical)

Geisler, Norman. "Freedom, Free Will, and Determinism." In *Evangelical Dictionary of Theology*, pp. 428-30. Grand Rapids: Baker, 1984. (Evangelical)

Henry, Carl F. H. "Image of God." In *Evangelical Dictionary of Theology*, pp. 545-48. Grand Rapids: Baker, 1984. (Evangelical)

Hoekema, Anthony. *Created in God's Image*, pp. 11-101. Grand Rapids: Eerdmans, 1986. (Reformed, Evangelical).

Niebuhr, Reinhold. *The Nature and Destiny of Man*, pp. 150-77. New York: Charles Scribner's, 1941. (Neoorthodox)

Notes for Chapter 2

1. This is borne out by its usage in Genesis alone. Whereas in Genesis 1:26 both words appear together without the Hebrew for "and" between them, "image" appears only in Genesis 1:27, "likeness" alone is found in Genesis 5:1, both appear again in Genesis 5:3 but in a different order, and finally in Genesis 9:6 only the word "image" is used. Thus their usage is interchangeable.

2. Francis Brown, S. R. Driver, and Charles Briggs, *Hebrew and English Lexicon of the Old Testament* (New York: Houghton Mifflin, 1907), p. 853.

3. Gordon J. Wenham, *Genesis 1-15*, Word Biblical Commentary (Waco, Tex.: Word, 1987), p. 29. There is no verb in biblical Hebrew to attest to its root meaning; the Arabic cognate supports the meaning "to cut." Another possibility from both Akkadian and Arabic is "to become dark." According to Wenham, "Its meaning must have been as opaque to them as it is to us."

4. Brown, Driver, and Briggs, *Hebrew and English Lexicon*, pp. 197-98.

5. Anthony Hoekema, *Created in God's Image* (Grand Rapids: Eerdmans, 1986), p. 13.

6. See A. H. Strong, *Systematic Theology* (Philadelphia: Judson, 1907), pp. 515-23, for a detailed development of those who have held some form of this view over the centuries.

7. Emil Brunner, *Man in Revolt* (Philadelphia: Westminster, 1948), pp. 102-5.

8. Karl Barth, *Church Dogmatics*, trans. Geoffrey Bromiley (Edinburgh: T. and T. Clark, 1956-60), 3:184, 214.

9. Leonard Verduin, *Somewhat Less Than God: The Biblical View of Man* (Grand Rapids: Eerdmans, 1970), p. 27.

10. G. C. Berkouwer, *Man: The Image of God*, in *Studies in Dogmatics* (Grand Rapids: Eerdmans, 1962), pp. 114-15.

11. H. D. McDonald, *The Christian View of Man* (Westchester, Ill.: Crossway, 1981), pp. 39-41.

12. Louis Berkhof, *Systematic Theology* (Grand Rapids: Eerdmans, 1941), pp. 208-10.

13. Strong, *Systematic Theology*, pp. 516-23.

14. Hoekema, *Created in God's Image*, pp. 82-83.

15. Thomas Aquinas, *Summa Theologica*, Q95.1.1 (New York: Benziger, 1947), pp. 482-83.

16. James Arminius, "Public Disputations," in *The Works of James Arminius*, trans. James and William Nichols (reprint, Grand Rapids: Baker, 1986), 2:151-53.

17. Ibid., 2:363.

18. Irenaeus, "Against Heresies," II.33.5; V.6.1, *The Ante-Nicene Fathers* (Grand Rapids: Eerdmans, 1969), 1:410-11; 1:532.

19. Franz Delitzsch, *A System of Biblical Psychology*, 2d ed., trans. Robert E. Wallis (Edinburgh: T. and T. Clark, 1867), pp. 247-66.

20. *The Scofield Reference Bible* (New York: Oxford U., 1909), n. 1 on 1 Thess. 5:23; *The New Scofield Reference Bible* (New York: Oxford U., 1967), n. 2 on 1 Thess. 5:23.

21. Berkhof, *Systematic Theology*, p. 192.

22. Strong, *Systematic Theology*, pp. 483-88.

23. Gordon H. Clark, *The Biblical Doctrine of Man* (Jefferson, Md.: Trinity Foundation, 1984), pp. 33-45.

24. Harry Emerson Fosdick, *The Modern Use of the Bible* (New York: Macmillan, 1933), pp. 99-100; see also William Newton Clarke, *An Outline of Christian Theology* (New York: Scribner, 1901), pp. 182-83.

25. John A. T. Robinson (*The Body* [London: SCM, 1952], p. 9) is a representative of the "biblical theology movement."

26. Millard Erickson, *Christian Theology* (Grand Rapids: Baker, 1986), pp. 530-39; see also a similar position called "psychosomatic unity," in Hoekema, *Created in God's Image*, pp. 217-26.

27. John Feinberg, "God Ordains All Things," in *Predestination and Free-will*, ed. David and Randall Basinger (Downers Grove: InterVarsity, 1986), pp. 20-24.

28. See Clark Pinnock, "God Limits His Knowledge," ibid., pp. 143-62.

29. I am indebted to the discussion by Hoekema, *Created in God's Image*, pp. 227-43.

3

HUMANITY'S FALLEN CONDITION

The Bible teaches that humanity's original created condition was altered by disobedience, an event first described in Genesis 3. Only the Bible describes such an event. Other religious books explain humanity's present condition in ways that are more favorable to its character. Certainly most scientists today consider humanity to be what evolution has made it; sin is an idea created by human beings to explain the unpleasant facts of reality.

Christianity cannot be understood apart from the biblical teaching of the Fall. That is a foundational concept; everything, such as the doctrine of salvation and the fact of death, is based on it. In fact, one senses the truthfulness of the Bible in its candid description of people as sinners. It is simply contrary to human nature to say the things about itself that the Bible says. Human tendency, on the contrary, is to deny sin and to think of the human species in a more complimentary way. Some people are evil, they would acknowledge, but these are exceptions.

THE GENESIS ACCOUNT

The approach of this text is to assume that the story of Adam and Eve is an actual historical event. Though some who deny this believe the story has some psychological validity, they think of it as merely a myth about how human beings first committed sin. Contrary to this, we will assume that it actually happened historically in time and space.

THE DIVINE PROHIBITION

Sometime after Adam had been created and placed in the Garden, God forbade him to eat of one particular tree, the "tree of the knowledge of good and evil" (Gen. 2:17). Everything else in the Garden was his to enjoy. There were no deprivations, and Adam and Eve had everything they needed and wanted. To go against this command was not to satisfy some need or add to their experience some pleasure the Creator had withheld. To break this command would be a simple act of rebellion with nothing actually to gain. It is not surprising, therefore, that some trickery would be involved in the first inducement to sin. The serpent provided this.

IDENTITY OF THE SERPENT

The Genesis story cryptically refers to the tempter as "the serpent." The only other point of identification is that he was "more crafty than any beast of the field which the Lord God had made" (Gen. 3:1). If we look carefully at this brief statement, we will notice that, although he is described as more crafty than the animals God had made, he is not necessarily described as one of them, i.e., another "wild animal." He is among them, but he may be an intruder.

Such a possibility may be supported by other biblical passages that have reference to this same creature. For one thing, the serpent is clearly identified in Revelation 12:9 and 20:2 as Satan. Jesus once referred to Satan as one who had fallen from heaven (Luke 10:18), and this implies that his original abode was not this earth. But here he is on earth, instigating the first sin that humanity was to commit.

Apart from explicit references to Satan in Scripture, two other passages have from early Christian times been applied to Satan's history that may fill in the gap of our knowledge about him. What caused his fall from heaven? How did he come into being? The passages that may answer those questions are Isaiah 14:12-15 and Ezekiel 28:11-19.

The Isaiah passage is addressed to the king of Babylon and the one in Ezekiel to the prince of Tyre. Many interpreters regard these passages as merely applying to the kings addressed, who, typical of the oriental exaggeration of their time, made claims about themselves far beyond reality.[1] I acknowledge the oriental exaggeration, but I believe that the very pride that caused these princes to enter into such fantasy is precisely the same thing that originates with Satan; thus they mirror Satan's original aspirations literally.

If the interpretation is true that Satan is actually in view in Isaiah 14 and Ezekiel 28,[2] then a fact is disclosed that contributes an insight to Adam's and Eve's temptation and Fall: Satan's fall was brought about by essentially the same sort of sin with which he tempted Eve: to be like God (see Ezek. 28:2 and Isa. 14:14; cf. Gen. 3:5).

THE STRATEGY OF THE TEMPTATION

Experience teaches all of us that Satan's approach in his temptation of Eve was a basic strategy that he has repeated in all of those he has tempted throughout history. It includes the following elements: perversion of the Word of God, denial of the Word of God, and an attack on the goodness of God.

Perversion of the Word of God. The opening words of Satan, "Did God really say?" was a challenge to the simple fact that God had indeed spoken and uttered the prohibition. If Satan can create doubt about whether God has given a command, he can weaken the will to resist. The next words, "You must not eat from any tree in the garden?" pervert God's original command, which forbade only one tree to be eaten from, and thus distorted the issue. They make God's command appear to be excessively strict and irrational, which further makes disobedience seem justified. This perversion paves the way for Eve's response in which she expresses a tinge of resentment toward God's prohibition by quoting beyond what He actually said: "You must not eat fruit from the tree that is in the middle of the garden, *and you must not touch it,* or you will die" (italics indicate Eve's addition).

Denial of the Word of God. The next words of Satan are a blatant denial of God's Word: "You will not surely die" (Gen. 3:4). He seems to say, "Even if God did say it, it won't happen." This simply defies God as if the sovereign Creator were impotent. Sometimes God's alleged weakness seems to be a reality when we do sin and at first seem to get away with it. When nothing immediately happens, we accept the illusion that nothing will. This sort of thing perpetuates further denial of God's Word. And so the disobedience goes on and on.

Attack on the goodness of God. "God knows," Satan alleges, "that when you eat of it your eyes will be opened, and you will be like God, knowing good and evil." These words imply that God is withholding something good, and thus they suggest that God is not altogether good. Eve's resistance is further broken down as she perceives that God is a cheat and to sin is the pursuit of something good. The belief that God is a tyrant who enjoys depriving His creatures of good things lies behind all temptation to break His laws.

THE PROCESS OF TEMPTATION

When it came to contemplating sin itself (the next stage of the temptation), Eve was tempted in three basic areas of life similar to those described in 1 John 2:15-16: "For everything in the world—the cravings of sinful man, the lust of his eyes and the boasting of what he has and does—comes not from the Father but from the world."[3] Note the correspondence of these three basic areas in the Genesis account: "When the woman saw that the fruit of the tree was good for food and pleasing to the eye, and also desirable for gaining wisdom, she took some and ate it" (Gen. 3:6).

The "cravings of sinful man" corresponds to the fact that the tree was good for food; in other words, this aspect of the temptation dealt with physical desires. The "lust of his eyes" corresponds to the fact that the fruit was pleasing to the eye, the area of enjoyment of beauty or perhaps materialistic desires. Finally, the "boasting of what he has and does" corresponds to the fact that the fruit was a means of gaining wisdom (or so she was told by Satan), the area of doing what one pleases.

Each of these areas involves a basic need of humanity built into it by creation, but each can be perverted by fulfilling it outside the design of the Creator. Therefore, temptation has that side of it in which there is a legitimate need, and this makes it compelling. The remedy, then, is to discover the legitimate way in which God intends that need to be met and opt for that, even if it means a temporary delay in fulfillment.

THE CONSEQUENCES OF SIN

Adam and Eve experienced two immediate consequences of their sin. First, there was a sense of shame. Genesis 3:7 says that their eyes were "opened" so that they realized they were naked. That seems to be a strange reaction from our point of view because they had never worn clothes anyway. But remember, shame brings a desire to hide, both figuratively and literally. We want to hide figuratively, for example, when we say "I could have crawled in a hole and pulled the dirt over me" because we are a-shamed. We want to hide literally by keeping away from those we have violated. Apparently Adam's and Eve's sense of nakedness was coupled with a desire to cover themselves, something they did with the fig leaves (Gen. 3:7).

Another even more obvious expression of shame is described in Genesis 3:8-11. Both Adam and Eve hid among the trees of the Garden when they heard the Lord approaching. Adam explains this to the Lord as shame for his nakedness. Sin had robbed the first humans of their innocence. The first unpleasant sensation had entered their lives as the result of sin.

Later in the Bible, sin is frequently described in terms of rebellion against God, and this often takes the form of escape from God so that God is excluded from the life of the rebel. To a large extent it is shame that lies behind this escape from God. We, too, participate in the consequences of sin as Adam did.

The second major consequence of sin was that Adam and Eve tried to avoid responsibility for their sin. Notice how both Adam and Eve had their individual ways of doing this. According to Genesis 3:11-13, Adam gave the excuse that the blame for his sin belonged to "the woman" God had given him. Eve, on the other hand, blamed her sin on the serpent who had deceived her. But "passing the buck" does not impress God. In the following verses He simply pronounces judgment on all of them.

The only way to deal with sin is to face up to one's responsibility in it. Probably the most common form of a person's failure to accept responsibility for the sinful condition is to blame it on the Creator ("I was made this way")

or on evolution ("I'm struggling with my animal instincts"
—as though animals were moral creatures).

THE JUDGMENT

Satan was the first target of God's curse, or judgment.
However, this text is concerned with the effects of sin on
mankind; thus we will pass over the serpent's curse and
discuss the curse on Eve and then the curse on Adam.

The curse on Eve. Genesis 3:16 indicates two aspects
of the curse on Eve: pain in childbearing, and a new relationship with her husband. The first of these is fairly obvious. It been the bane of womanhood all these centuries.
The second aspect, the new relationship with Adam, has
given rise to a number of differing interpretations and even
touches on the modern controversy of the role of women
in the home, church, and society.

The first set of interpretations deals with the meaning
of the words "your desire will be for your husband." Perhaps the oldest interpretation is that the desire is sexual;[4]
the context of childbearing, after all, lends support to this.
Understood thus, the thought is that the pain of childbirth
is offset by sexual desire, which keeps the children coming
in spite of the prospect of pain.

Slightly different from this interpretation of the word
"desire" is that the desire is for intimate relationship, a bit
broader than sex but including it.[5] If this interpretation is
accepted, the meaning is that this broader relationship
more than compensates for the pain of childbirth.

Yet another interpretation of the word "desire" is that
it means "desire to dominate."[6] This phrase in Genesis 3:16
corresponds with the Hebrew construction found in Genesis 4:7 in which sin, "crouching at the door," desired Cain,
who had failed to please God in his offering and was
"downcast" and evidently bitterly jealous of his brother
Abel. Sin is figuratively seen in this interpretation as desir-

ing to *dominate* Cain if he failed to "do what is right" (presumably offer the proper sacrifice). Thus, the curse on Eve is that she will desire to dominate Adam, and that has been the case with womankind throughout history.

This latter interpretation suffers from the fact that "desire" is not explicitly said to be desire to dominate. Probably what it means is desire to "have," which would fit both contexts rather well.[7] Thus, the "desire" of Genesis 3:16 is probably best understood as desire for relationship in which the wife naturally tends to build her life around her husband.

This brings us to the problem of the interpretation of the words "he [Adam] will rule over you." That this implies a change of the former relationship seems obvious, but the question is, What was the old relationship, and what is the new one?

The modern evangelical feminists who accept the full authority of Scripture are convinced that Eve's relationship to Adam was one of partnership, an interpretation of the words "helper suitable for him" (Gen. 2:18).[8] This, they believe, was an equal partnership (egalitarian). According to this view the Fall brought about a change in which Adam will "rule over" Eve, an unequal, if not oppressive, relationship.[9] Christian marriage and the roles of men and women in the church should restore the original equality lost by the Fall, something implied by the words of Galatians 3:28: "There is neither . . . male nor female . . . in Christ Jesus."

The more traditional interpretation recognizes that the words "he will rule over you" express a more dominating relationship of Adam over Eve.[10] But traditionalists believe that the original relationship was not a strict equality in role but that Eve was created "for" Adam to "help" him, and that this suggests a subordinate role, although she of course is equal to the man is every other respect except possibly physical strength. Christianity indeed is intended to restore this original role relationship, not abolish all male authority in the home and in the church. Women, they believe, experienced a decided improvement in status both over the consequences of the Fall and over the harsher chauvinism that came about by man's sinfulness through the ages since the Fall.

The curse on Adam. The judgment on Adam pertains to the physical creation and his new relationship to it. Genesis 3:17-19 contains a curse on the ground and the necessity of "painful toil" to cultivate it. Inedible things such as thorns would begin to grow, making cultivation necessary. The paradise of the Garden was history. Work, however, probably contains what is necessary to keep the sin nature in check. A prominent theme in the book of Proverbs, for example, is the benefit of honest labor: "Lazy hands make a man poor, but diligent hands bring wealth" (Prov. 10:4).

The more significant aspect of the judgment on Adam was the pronouncement of physical death. The Lord tells him, "You will eat your food until you return to the ground since from it you were taken; for dust you are and to dust you will return" (Gen. 3:19). The death that was promised in Genesis 2:17 is now a factor in his body, aging him and bringing about decay and dissolution.

The expulsion. Genesis 3:22-24 puts the final touch on the story of the Fall of humanity by explaining that another kind of death—spiritual death—also occurred for Adam and Eve. By driving them from the Garden, God brings about a separation in relationship. No longer will God be available to humanity to fellowship with them, no longer will they talk together "in the cool of the day" (Gen. 3:8). Humanity's alienation is complete. God will speak with people in selected ways and times, but there will not be that happy proximity, and future generations will grow farther and farther from Him, with the notable exceptions of those touched by divine grace, such as Noah, Enoch, and Moses. Someday, of course, redemption by Jesus Christ will bring about the full restoration of humanity, when death and sin are abolished (Rev. 22:3).

CONCLUSION

Genesis 3 teaches the following significant facts: (1) humanity, not God, is responsible for bringing sin into the world and with it death and the corruption of nature; (2) the temptation appealed to the basic needs of humanity and took a pattern that continues today whenever a person is tempted; (3) judgment occurred in which the original order of things was radically altered: pain in childbirth, frustration in male-female relations, pain and toil for survival, and both physical and spiritual death.

THE ROMANS ACCOUNT

One of the most complete and prolific accounts of the human condition is found in Romans 1:18–3:20. In order to explain salvation by faith, Paul must first show the human race's utter need for such a salvation.

THE SUPPRESSED KNOWLEDGE OF GOD

Paul opens with the fact that the human race is facing the "wrath" of God. "Wrath" is righteous anger toward sin and arises out of the absolute holiness of God. Eventually it will cause the destruction of all disobedient persons (1 Thess. 1:5-10), but at present it is "being revealed from heaven [God]" that the world might be warned and repent. Those who reject this gracious warning by God, which comes in various ways (e.g., conscience, gospel preaching, biblical history), will ultimately be assigned to the lake of fire (Rev. 20:15).

This wrath is deserved, Paul continues, because humanity actually has a knowledge of God that it is suppressing. Presumably if people responded to this truth as they should, they would be led into belief in the gospel, which would save them from wrath.[11]

What this knowledge of God is. Romans 1:19-20 describes a general revelation of God to all people, whatever their knowledge of revelation in the Bible may be. Romans 2:14-15 adds somewhat to this description. The first passage describes this knowledge as "eternal power and divine nature."

The first of these, eternal power, is easy enough to understand. The greatness and magnitude of creation attests to a cause that must be greater, since all causes in our physical realm are sufficient to their effects, i.e., great enough or powerful enough to bring them about. To say that the universe came about by chance and from nothing or to say that the material universe is itself eternal is to ignore the lesson of our observation of lesser phenomena in the world around us.

The second thing revealed about God from the physical universe is God's divine nature. This word seems to contain the idea of attributes or whatever makes God what He is. The Greek word it translates is *theiotes*, which can also be translated "deity," or "that which makes deity what it is."[12] What qualities of deity are revealed by the physical realm? Christians may be tempted to assume that everything to be known about God has to come from the Bible simply because we ourselves have always had it. Evidently the Bible is not the only source of information about God.

Some examples of divine attributes revealed in nature are intelligence, love, and moral nature (holiness). The great design and presence of natural law suggest intelligence. Love is implied by the possibility of our physical needs being provided for, and morality is best explained by a law-giver who establishes what is right and wrong. It is true that these are often explained by humanists in other ways, but the point here is that if we wish to imagine what

God is like, assuming there is a God, it is reasonable to conclude that He has these attributes, because if the universe has a cause, He must be like this to have caused it.

The other passage, Romans 2:14-15, zeroes in on this moral idea of God, for it speaks of humanity's conscience, or sensitivity to morality. If we believe this conscience has a divine cause, we logically predicate conscience or moral perfection to God. Though the passage says that no person is true to his conscience, the mere presence of something in him that attests to morality cannot easily be explained away, especially when that conscience drives a person to do some things that are unselfish or sacrificial.

Human decline. When a person suppresses the truth that is available, it leads to a step-by-step decline in moral capacity. Evidently the opposite of suppressing the truth about God is, according to Romans 1:21, to glorify God and give thanks to Him. This is the same as worshiping God. A human being is a worshiping creature, and if one object of worship is abandoned (in this case, God), a vacuum is created so that some other form of worship rushes in to take its place. That which historically took the place of acknowledging or worshiping God was idolatry: the worship of "images made to look like mortal man and birds and animals and reptiles" (1:23).

This, then, must be a brief history of human religions. Such religions go from God to reptiles. Usually evolutionists teach that it must have been the other way around, that primitive people worshiped such foolish things as reptiles and spirits in various objects and gradually improved in their religions until now they believe in one supreme, personal deity. Perhaps one day even the idea of personality is something that will be eventually abandoned for the idea of a Supreme Power, or Force. This, in fact, is an idea growing in popularity.

If we today—or at any other point in the past—have a more lofty concept of God than some depraved peoples, it is by the grace of God's educating us to His biblical revelation through the influence of the gospel and missions. Otherwise all of us would right now be bowing down to some detestable object. Only grace, not great intelligence, overcomes the natural tendency of humanity to worship in such ignorance.

Following Paul's description of human worship as turning from the true God to idols, three further stages of decline are set forth in the remaining part of Romans 1. Humanity does not remain morally and spiritually in a status quo position. Things get worse, much worse.

From idolatry a human being descends first to sexual immorality. This occurs as God "gives him over." What this implies is that up to a point God restrains a person's natural tendencies, but when a form of sin runs a certain course, he allows him to continue on along a prescribed path of consequences. It is not clear just why, but idolatry turns to sexual sin, a fact illustrated by the fertility cults of the ancient world, which entailed prostitution as an act of worship.

The first form taken by sexual sin is heterosexual but contrary to the divine plan of sex within the institution of marriage, here called "sexual impurity" (1:24-25). The second divine "giving over" leads to homosexuality, called "shameful lusts" (1:26-27). Furthermore, it is described as "unnatural," attesting to the fact that homosexuality is contrary to the creation order God established between male and female.[13] For this reason it is regarded as sin throughout the Bible (see Lev. 18:22).

The third and last divine "giving over" is to a "depraved mind," i.e., a mind incapable of distinguishing between good and evil and inclined totally toward evil. The condition described in Romans 1:28-32 reminds one of the point to which humanity came in Genesis 6:5-6: "The Lord saw how great man's wickedness on the earth had become, and that every inclination of the thoughts of his heart was only evil all the time." In fact, this moral description in Romans 1 may actually chart the course of events from the Fall of Genesis 3 to the period before the Flood in Genesis 6-9. History then and since seems to run in such a cycle; it may be possible to plot the moral position of a society according to what prevails at a given time in relation to Romans 1. In other words, the widespread practice of homosexuality signals the fact that total moral anarchy may be near, and when moral anarchy runs its course, divine judgment comes—unless, of course, God graciously interrupts the madness by revival.

Conclusion. According to Romans 1 people decline as divine grace is gradually withdrawn. The decline begins initially when a person fails to acknowledge God and departs from true worship and various forms of human religion take over, which, of course, are merely forms of idolatry. From there God allows humanity to descend to sexual immorality, then sexual perversion, and finally to total inability to perform morally.

That leaves one final perplexing question: Why does God withdraw His gracious restraint and allow a person to plunge into such depths of depravity? Paul does not answer that question here, but the answer can be surmised from the fact that Paul teaches the possibility of repentance for anyone elsewhere. What God may be providing through His "giving over" to sin is the occasion for repentance. In other words, seeing the consequences of sin stimulates in some the repugnance toward sin that leads to repentance. Though it varies from person to person, resistance to God is a powerful force for which drastic circumstances are sometimes the only cure.

Therefore, the process of humanity's decline may not be always inevitable. There are Christians who can testify to having come to repentance and faith in Jesus Christ at every stage of decline described in Romans 1 (1 Cor. 6:9-11).

THE UNIVERSALITY OF GUILT

Regardless of one's religious background and knowledge, or lack of such, he or she is guilty before God. In Paul's day there were a number of religions, but Paul saw the world as essentially only two groups: Jew and Gentile. The Jew had his Bible, and all the varieties of Gentiles were characterized simply by the fact that they did not have the Bible and thus were ignorant of many things about God. The interesting fact that Paul brings out starting with Romans 2 is that no one, regardless of his religious knowledge, is at any advantage so far as his being guilty is concerned. The same suppression of truth and rebellion toward God appear among all kinds of people; they merely take different forms.

The pagan, or Gentile. Paul has already established the case against the pagan world—the world without the Bible —in the first chapter of Romans. The pagan has a knowledge of God, but that knowledge does no good, for he or she turns his back on it. Suppression takes a person further and further into sin. The pagan is without excuse and cannot plead ignorance.

The moralist. It is not clear whether Romans 2:1-16 is dealing with the Jew or someone else. The Jew is not addressed explicitly until 2:17, but what is said here could be said of him. However, because of the generalized way Paul talks about this person, the statement he makes in 2:14-15 about Gentiles doing the things of the law because of their conscience though not having the law, and the fact that the Jew is not mentioned by name until 2:17, support the possibility that another kind of Gentile, the "moralist," is Paul's subject in 2:1-16.

The moralist, like all humankind created in God's image, has the law of God written on his conscience, but, unlike many counterparts, the moralist is making some attempt to follow that law. This attempt to keep the law of

conscience is neither successful nor worthy. Paul says flat-
ly, "At whatever point you judge the other, you are con-
demning yourself, because you who pass judgment do the
same things" (2:1). This implies more than mere weakness;
even motives cannot be worthy, even when he or she does
what appears to be something unselfish and noble. This is
a fact brought out in the third chapter. "There is no one
righteous, not even one; there is no one who understands,
no one who seeks God" (vv. 10-11). Unless good is done for
God, it is not really good. Ironically, this "not really good"
is possible because of a form of grace God exercises in behalf of all human beings, a grace that prevents them from
always being as bad as they might be.

Moralists have a form of the "law" of God "written on
their hearts" (2:15). This is probably part of the image of
God, a universal sense of right or wrong. Everyone has a
sense of justice, and this in itself can lead to noble deeds,
but since it is not a sense of justice that desires to uphold
God's standards for the sake of God Himself, it is not pure-
ly motivated. This has misled many to think of humanity
as being essentially good, not depraved. Depraved people
can do good and noble deeds, but they do not do them for
the sake of God.

The Jew. The guilt of the Jew, the person with the law
of God, is somewhat like the guilt of the moralist in that the
Jew does not practice what he or she preaches (2:21-24).
The biggest difference, besides the obvious fact that each
has the revealed and written law of God, is that each brags
about a relationship with God (2:17). Thus, when he or she
fails to obey but hypocritically pretends to obey, each
brings reproach upon God (2:24).

Besides this, the Jew's peculiar form of suppression of
the truth is a bit more sophisticated. This is cleverly exposed by Paul when, after a series of questions asking if the
Jew has obeyed certain things he has taught others, he
asks, "You who abhor idols, do you rob temples?" (2:22).

You would have expected Paul to ask instead, "You who abhor idols, do you also *worship* in temples?" to preserve the pattern of the previous questions. The Jew would have glibly answered, "Of course I do not worship in temples!" But the way the question is worded, a unique form of idolatry is exposed to his legalistic readers. Religious sinners have a subtle way of committing sin that is not considered to be sin by a devious process of rationalization. Modern Christians often do similar things.

How sin spreads to the human race. Most agree that all humans are sinners, but not all agree as to just how this happens. Such a question as this involves how Romans 5:12 should be interpreted: "Therefore, just as sin entered the world through one man, and death through sin, and in this way death came to all men, because all sinned . . ."

The *Pelagian* view, a view named after Pelagius, a British monk who lived during the fifth century A.D., interprets Romans 5:12 as something that happens when an individual actually commits sin through the influence of other sinners, not because that person is born with a sinful tendency. He believed that it was theoretically possible for a person not to sin in the right environment.[14]

The *Arminian* view generally holds that, as the result of Adam's sin, every human being receives a corrupted, sinful nature that affects the physical and intellectual part but not his will. He can will to do good and, with the help of prevenient grace, accomplish what he wills. But the weaknesses of the flesh and the perversion of the mind usually lead him toward sin.[15]

The *Calvinist* view takes the most extreme interpretation of Romans 5:12. Every part of humanity, including the will, has been corrupted by Adam's sin directly due to a solidarity of the human race as it existed in Adam. Such a direct imputation (transfer of sin and guilt) is borne out, the Calvinist believes, by the verses that follow, in which what Adam does directly affects the whole human race and what Christ does also directly affects those who believe (5:13-21).[16]

Conclusion: Humanity's utter depravity. Paul admits that the Jew had a kind of advantage (3:1-2), but it was the advantage of certain privileges, not any superior righteousness. The Jew had "the very words of God" (3:2) and, thus, by grace the possibility of more perfect obedience if he had faith (3:3).

Paul's conclusion is "that Jews and Gentiles alike are all under sin" (3:9). What follows is a selection of Old Testament passages that further describe the utter depravity that characterizes all humankind. None is righteous, none seeks God, none avoids the sin of the tongue, none avoids violence, and none fears God (3:10-18).

How are these statements to be understood? As the ravings of some disillusioned prophet? The fact is that there indeed are those who appear to be righteous, who seek God, who guard their tongues, who hate violence, and who seem to fear God—those who are not even professing Christians. Many of us who now are believers can testify to having sought after God before we found Him.

What, then, does Paul mean? What Paul means is that here is what man does apart from any grace from God. Leave sinners to themselves and they will go the opposite way from God. Leave sinners to themselves and none will ever be saved. God must take the initiative and seek after a person (see Romans 10, where He must send the messenger so that the sinner can hear the message and believe).

Perhaps a further point of clarification would be helpful. In my opinion, even those unbelievers who do good and are noble are doing what conforms to the law of God (see 2:14-15), but they are not doing this good for the glory of God. In other words, they have their own personal reasons—and, I would say, ultimately selfish reasons—for what they do. Only that which arises out of faith truly pleases God (14:23).

That God must take the initiative and seek after a person has been understood in two different ways (whichever of these two is accepted determines how he interprets the rest of the Bible so far as biblical anthropology is concerned). (1) The strict Calvinist view is that people are in total rebellion against God and thus will not seek (indeed *cannot* seek) God.[17] But the Calvinist says that the initiative God takes is in the form of effectual grace given only to the elect, not to all. The reason God does not give such grace to all is a divine mystery not to be challenged or questioned; rather, we must instead ask why God saves any. (2) The Arminian takes the passage as a description of total depravity, but he believes that the initiative of God means that he gives prevenient grace to all so that their wills are not in bondage as they otherwise would be. Thus all are able to exercise faith if they would, though not all do.[18] My own conclusion is that depravity must be understood in the strictest sense to be total unwillingness or inability, and, since there is no explicit evidence for "prevenient" grace anywhere in the Bible other than by inference, that "effectual grace" is necessary for sinners to believe, a grace given only to the elect. When people refuse the invitation, they do so completely upon their own volition and are fully responsible for the choice they make.

OTHER BIBLICAL EVIDENCE FOR DEPRAVITY

Though we have concentrated on the Genesis passage of the Fall and the Romans passage about depravity, the idea of human depravity pervades the entire Bible. Just a few scattered examples will be sufficient to demonstrate this.

Genesis 6:5: "The Lord saw how great man's wickedness on the earth had become, and that every inclination of the thoughts of his heart was only evil all the time." It is true that, whereas this passage describes man at his lowest decline in history, it nevertheless describes the potential in all human beings.

Genesis 8:21: "The Lord smelled the pleasing aroma [Noah's sacrifice] and said in his heart: 'Never again will I curse the ground because of man, even though every inclination of his heart is evil from childhood.'" This is a promise never again to bring a flood as a punishment on sin. Humanity's inner nature, nevertheless, would certainly deserve it.

1 Kings 8:46-47, 49: "When they sin against you—for there is no one who does not sin—and you become angry with them and give them over to the enemy, who takes them captive to his own land, far away or near; and if they have a change of heart . . . and repent and plead with you in the land of their conquerors and say, 'We have sinned,' . . . from heaven . . . hear their prayer and their plea." Solomon did not say, "*If* they sin," but, "*When* they sin," an absolute certainty.

Job 14:4: "Who can bring what is pure from the impure? No one!" Job's reference to "impure," of course, is to humanity (see 14:1).

Psalm 130:3: "If you, O Lord, kept a record of sins, O Lord, who could stand?" To "keep a record" means to count a person's sins against him no matter what.

Ecclesiastes 7:20: "There is not a righteous man on earth who does what is right and never sins." There may be righteous people on earth, but not in the absolute sense of sinlessness. What righteousness occurs is by the grace of God.

Ephesians 2:3: "All of us lived among them [unregenerated mankind] at one time, gratifying the cravings of our sinful nature and following its desires and thoughts. Like the rest, we were by nature objects of wrath." Paul probably intends the words "by nature" to mean "by birth."

1 John 1:8, 10: "If we claim to be without sin, we deceive ourselves and the truth is not in us. . . . If we claim we

have not sinned, we make him out to be a liar." The first claim is to lack of a sin nature, the second to acts of sin. Comprehensively, no one is without either, and this is addressed to regenerated believers.

EFFECTS OF THE FALL ON THE IMAGE OF GOD

Some theologians such as G. C. Berkouwer[19] and Arthur Custance[20] take the view that when Adam sinned in the Garden he lost the image of God. It usually follows in their theology that the image is restored when a person is regenerated. There are at least two flaws in this theory.

The first flaw is that such a view fails to do justice to Genesis 9:6, which explains that murderers should be put to death because the victim is created in the image of God; in other words, an attack on the life of a human being is an attack on the image of God in him. If the image of God were no longer in him, this verse would be meaningless (see also Gen. 5:1 and Ps. 8:5).

The second flaw is that it may assume an inadequate concept of what the image of God is. If, for example, the image includes, as I have defined it, a sense of morality, then this would contradict Romans 2, which teaches that the unregenerate has the law of God within his conscience.

The best way to describe the effect of sin on the image of God is that it is corrupted or marred in some way. For example, if part of the image of God is humanity's ability to fellowship with God, then the Fall has affected it in this respect. Through humanity's personality, fellowship is possible, but the Fall has caused the human race to be alienated against God so that it no longer wants to have a relationship with God—at least with the God of the Bible. Religion is actually a substitute for true relationship with God.

Another—and probably primary—way in which the image of God is affected by the Fall is in a person's desire to obey God. By creation, humanity has the capacity to obey God, but the Fall made people into rebels. A person knows (at least in his conscience) what is right, but has no desire, for the sake of God, to obey. A person may appear to "obey," but instead of really obeying God, he is doing what is right for some ulterior reason, usually a selfish one. This explains how moral people can exist apart from biblical faith.

THE REMEDY FOR HUMANITY'S FALLEN CONDITION

It is not customary for books on biblical anthropology to discuss human salvation in any detail, for this falls classically into a separate division known as soteriology, the doctrine of salvation. Nevertheless, a few remarks are appropriate here, because salvation appears to do more than merely restore a person to the original condition before the Fall.

Justification by faith in Jesus Christ and His finished sacrifice on the cross restores humanity to more than "innocence," assuming that word adequately describes Adam by his original creation. Evidence for this is found in Paul's letter to the Romans.

Having described in Romans 5:12-14 how sin permeated the whole human race when Adam first sinned, Paul begins Romans 5:15 with the following words:

> But the gift is not like the trespass. For if the many died by the trespass of the one man, how much more did God's grace and the gift that came by the grace of the one man, Jesus Christ, overflow to the many! Again, the gift of God is not like the result of the one man's sin: The judgment followed one sin and brought condemnation, but the gift followed many trespasses and brought justification. For if, by the trespass of the one man, death reigned through that

one man, how much more will those who receive God's abundant provision of grace and of the gift of righteousness reign in life through the one man, Jesus Christ. (5:15-17)

Notice the words "not like," and "much more." These imply that consequences of Christ's obedience go beyond the consequences of Adam's disobedience and place justified humanity in a superior position than creation status. This superior position is called "justified" or "righteous." This means that justified humanity has a status before God that cannot be altered (8:28-30), unlike the situation before the Fall, in which sin was able to alter humanity's position before God.

Another remedy for humanity's Fall is regeneration, an act by the Holy Spirit in which a person is granted new spiritual life and shares in God's nature (John 3:5-8). What this gives a person beyond what Adam had is a disposition toward obedience to God. Adam was "righteous" in the sense that he was without sin by his creation, but he was not inclined either toward sin or righteousness (see chap. 2).

The inclination toward righteousness, which regenerated humanity has, does not guarantee right actions due to the presence of another rebellious force within what Paul calls the "flesh" (see chap. 4), a kind of remnant of sin left from the Fall. Instead, the indwelling Holy Spirit, who is given at salvation, motivates and empowers in this inclination.

Finally, the ultimate solutions for the Fall are growth toward holiness (sanctification) and final perfection (glorification). This latter final act will also bring the full redemption of the body, a total restoration of the effects of the Fall on the body.

For Further Thought

1. Discuss what the real motives might be for people who do the following noble deeds: one who gives to charity; a medical doctor who goes to a primitive area to practice his medicine; an unbeliever who goes into the ministry; one who gives his life in order to save another's.

2. Show how the temptation to indulge in pornography might follow the pattern of temptation Eve experienced.

3. Using the stages of decline described in Romans 1, discuss where you think our present society might be.

4. How would you go about explaining the idea of human depravity in simple language that a person with relatively little education could understand?

For Further Reading

Berkouwer, G. C. *Man: The Image of God*, pp. 119-93. Grand Rapids: Eerdmans, 1962.

Demarest, Bruce A. "Fall of Man." In *Evangelical Dictionary of Theology*. Grand Rapids: Baker, 1984.

Erickson, Millard. *Christian Theology*, pp. 601-58. Grand Rapids: Baker, 1985.

Hoekema, Anthony A. *Created in God's Image*, pp. 112-67. Grand Rapids: Eerdmans, 1986.

Ryrie, Charles C. "Total Depravity." In *Evangelical Dictionary of Theology*. Grand Rapids: Baker, 1984.

NOTES FOR CHAPTER 3

1. Franz Delitzsch (*Biblical Commentary on the Prophecies of Isaiah* [Grand Rapids: Eerdmans, 1965], 1:312-13) takes the view that in Isaiah 14 the king of Babylon is solely in view and is typically exaggerating.

2. Charles L. Feinberg (*The Prophecy of Ezekiel* [Chicago: Moody, 1969], pp. 161-64) is an example of a commentator who sees that Satan is partly in view as the power behind the prince of Tyre.

3. When Jesus was tempted, He also was approached by way of these same three areas of human need. Compare them from the account in Luke 4:1-13.

4. C. F. Keil (*Commentary on the Old Testament: The Pentateuch* [Grand Rapids: Eerdmans, 1978], 1:103) calls it "desire" and "urge."

5. Gilbert Bilezikian (*Beyond Sex Roles* [Grand Rapids: Baker, 1986], pp. 227-28) sees the "desire" as "desire to *have*," i. e., "intimacy."

6. Susan Foh (*Women and the Word of God* [Grand Rapids: Baker, 1979], pp. 67-69) believes it is a desire to "dominate," or overcome.

7. Bilezikian, *Beyond Sex Roles*, pp. 227-28.

8. Ibid., p. 217.

9. Millard Erickson (*Christian Theology* [Grand Rapids: Baker, 1986], pp. 546-47) calls attention to the fact that the Hebrew word translated "rule over" in almost all English translations is given an alternate meaning in Brown, Driver, and Briggs's *Hebrew and English Lexicon of the Old Testament* (New York: Houghton Mifflin, 1907), p. 617: "to be like." In this particular context, he contends, such a meaning would fit well and would mean that Adam would experience similar pain or anguish as Eve. Such a translation would solve the problem of the meaning of "rule over" by eliminating it altogether, but neither the Hebrew scholars nor the history of interpretation is on the side of such a meaning.

10. An example of the traditional view can be found in C. F. Keil, *Commentary on the Old Testament: The Pentateuch*, p. 103.

11. This is an inference based on Romans 10:14-15, which requires that in order to believe, someone must hear the gospel, and that God must send one to preach the gospel. Anyone who indeed does "call on the name of the Lord" (Rom. 10:13) must therefore be the recipient of the grace of God, for no one ordinarily seeks for God (3:11). Arminians believe that all human beings have received such grace (called "prevenient" grace), whereas Calvinists believe only the "elect" receive such grace (called "effectual grace").

12. C. E. B. Cranfield (*The International Critical Commentary: A Critical and Exegetical Commentary on the Epistle to the Romans* [Edinburgh: T. and T. Clark, 1975], 1:115) says *theiotes* denotes "the divine nature and [its] properties."

13. Homosexuals interpret the word "unnatural" as promiscuous homosexuality, an act that therefore does not apply to "constituted" homosexuals as they consider themselves to be. Actually Paul uses the word in reference to creation, a use confirmed by the general context. In Scripture the *act* of homosexuality is condemned; there are not "natural" and "unnatural" kinds of homosexuality.

14. Pelagius, "De Peccato Original, 14," in *Documents of the Christian Church*, ed. Henry Bettenson (New York: Oxford U., 1947), p. 75.

15. James Arminius, "Public Disputations," in *Works of James Arminius*, 2:375.

16. John Calvin, *Institutes of the Christian Religion*, II.1.5, ed. John T. McNeill; trans. Ford Lewis Battles (Philadelphia: Westminster, 1960), pp. 246-55.

17. Ibid., II.1.8.

18. James Arminius, "Public Disputations," in *Works of James Arminius*, 2:375. He calls it "the absence of original righteousness only."

19. G. C. Berkouwer, *Man, The Image of God* (Grand Rapids: Eerdmans, 1962), pp. 119-47.

20. Arthur C. Custance, *Man in Adam and in Christ* (Grand Rapids: Zondervan, 1975), pp. 114-26.

4

THE BIBLICAL WORDS FOR HUMANITY'S INNER BEING

There is a kind of biblical "psychology" involved in the words the Bible uses to refer to humanity's inner being that in itself can tell us something about the biblical concept of anthropology. What this involves is an expansion of sorts on the image of God concept we defined in chapter 2. What follows will be a brief study of the Old and New Testament terms used to describe humanity's inner nature.[1]

SOUL[2]

The Hebrew word for soul is *nepesh*, whereas the Greek term is *psyche* (or *psuche*), from which English derives such words as *psychic* and *psychology*. The Hebrew root of *nepesh* is "to breathe," and similarly the basic meaning of the Greek *psyche* is "wind" or "breath."

The Greek Old Testament (Septuagint or LXX) uses the Greek *psyche* more than nine hundred times, and most of these occurrences are translations of the Hebrew *nepesh*. *Nepesh* has a range of meaning that includes the whole person, a unity of the body, will, and life, and emphasizes personal desire or inclination. Seldom is it used in reference to God, since God does not have cravings and appetites common to humanity or life that is limited by death.

In the New Testament, *psyche* appears mostly in the narrative parts, especially the synoptic gospels and the book of Acts. For example, in Acts 27:22 it means "the life," in Acts 3:23 the "whole person," in Acts 14:2 a place of feeling, in Mark 8:35-36 the "supreme good," and in Matthew 10:28 it is used in contrast with the body. In the writings of Paul it means "true life" (Phil. 2:20) and the whole person (Rom. 2:9), but Paul never uses *psyche* of life that survives death; in such cases he prefers the word "spirit" (Gk. *pneuma*). The rest of the New Testament follows these usages fairly closely. To sum up: the New Testament usage of *psyche* is the seat of life, the inner life, person, or personality.

In the writings of Paul a variant of *psyche* is found: *psychikos*, which is used in contrast to *pneumatikos* ("spiritual") and means "natural" (see 1 Cor. 2:14). Also, it is used to contrast the present physical, mortal body with the future resurrection body in 1 Corinthians 15:44.

The word "soul" in the Bible is thus generally the term for natural life. When used of humanity, it means human life and relates a person to animal life. Modern usage has made "soul" the eternal part of man.[3] For example, in evangelism we talk about "saving souls" and warn people about forfeiting their "souls" for the world. The Bible tends to use another word for this eternal aspect of humanity —"spirit"—although ultimately humanity is thought of as a unity of the physical and spiritual after the resurrection takes place (see chap. 2 and the discussion of trichotomy, dichotomy, monism, and unity).

SPIRIT[4]

The Old Testament word for "spirit" is *ruah*, whereas in the New Testament it is *pneuma*, from which English gets such words as "pneumatic" and "pneumonia." *Ruah* essentially means air in motion. From this come the meanings of breath, vital powers, spirit, feelings, and will. *Pneu-*

ma is almost always the translation of *ruah* in the LXX, and in the New Testament it means about the same thing.

In the New Testament there are certain emphases of "spirit." In the synoptic gospels it is the seat of perceptions and feelings (Mark 2:8), in Luke-Acts it is that which in humanity survives death (Luke 8:55). In Paul's writings "spirit" refers to human psychological functions (1 Cor. 7:34), the whole person (2 Cor. 2:13), and the "new I" of the person of faith (1 Cor. 5:3). John never uses "spirit" of human beings, but other books such as James 2:26 use it of that which gives life to the body, and 1 Peter 3:19 uses it of the dead.

What is the distinction between "spirit" and "soul"? In the Old Testament "spirit" is humanity's rational and immortal life, reason, will, and conscience. It is related to the divine image in human beings. On the other hand, "soul" in the Old Testament is related to humanity's emotions and desires; it refers to his distinctive personality.[5] "Soul" is the whole person of emotions; "spirit" is related to God as well as the whole person, humanity as "empowered" by God.[6]

MIND[7]

The Old Testament has no equivalent for the Greek word *nous* ("mind"). Instead, the Hebrew word for "heart" is used by the Old Testament to express the functions of mind. Furthermore, *nous* is used mostly by Paul in reference to humanity.

Though the word *nous* lacks precise meaning, it nevertheless is distinct from "spirit" and "soul" in the New Testament. For example, it seems to mean "mind" or "disposition" in Romans 1:28; Ephesians 4:17; and 1 Timothy 6:5. It means "practical reason," or the moral consciousness that determines will and action in Romans 7:23. In

Luke 24:45 and Revelation 13:18 it is the "understanding" or faculty of knowledge. Finally, in Romans 14:5 it is simply "thought," "judgment," or "resolve."

A related word is *dianoia*, which means "ability to think," "faculty of knowledge," or "understanding." Though *dianoia* was used frequently in Greek philosophy as the organ of thought that comprehends the world and existence and orders and controls everything, its New Testament usage is quite different and corresponds with its usage in the LXX. For example, in Jeremiah 31:33 it is parallel to "heart."

In Christian usage *nous* is right understanding that leads to a right attitude of mind. The heathen have a foolish attitude of mind (Eph. 4:17, 23), whereas the Holy Spirit upholds and fills the mind of the Christian.

Another group of words related to "mind" are *phrenes* and its antonyms *aphron* and *aphrosyne*. *Phrenes* means "mind" or "understanding" and is a synonym for *nous*. In the New Testament this group of words is found most often in verbal forms, but in 1 Corinthians 14:20, the noun *phresin* means "reason." Paul uses its opposite, *aphron*, in Romans 2:20 as "foolish." The Old Testament has equivalents translated by *phrenes* and *aphron* in *hakam* and *bin*.

CONSCIENCE[8]

As it was in the case of "mind," the Old Testament has no exact equivalent of the New Testament Greek word for "conscience": *suneidesis*. Here again, functions of the "conscience" are attributed by the Old Testament to the "heart."

In Romans 2:15 *suneidesis* stands alongside "heart" and "thoughts" as a faculty that enables the pagan world to live a life that corresponds to the Jews who have the written law. The conscience awakens awareness of the law written on their heart. Thus, the conscience "appears . . . as a court of appeal which is not able to promulgate any statutes (for only God can do this) but is able to deliver judgments on the cases before it."[9]

The Christian conscience is transformed by faith in Jesus Christ. The Greeks saw conscience as something bad, by which one felt accused *after* he had done wrong. To the believer the conscience is motivated by his realization of his standing in Christ and thus acts as a *preventative* of sin.

HEART[10]

Several terms are associated in the Old Testament with the Hebrew *leb* (or *lebab*): "heart," "feelings," "wish," "reason," and decisions of the will.[11] In these abstract meanings it became the richest biblical term for the totality of humanity's inner or immaterial nature. In the Old Testament virtually every immaterial function of humanity is attributed to the "heart." Also strange to modern readers is the frequent use of "kidneys" in connection with the heart (Ps. 7:9).

The New Testament *kardia* coincides closely with the Old Testament understanding of the term: the inner life, center of the personality and the place in which God reveals himself to human beings. For example, it is the center of physical life (Luke 21:34) and the spiritual life (2 Cor. 3:14). Sin can dominate the heart (Mark 7:21). God alone can reveal the hidden things in the heart (1 Cor. 4:5), and the heart is the place where God arouses and creates faith (Rom. 6:17). It is the seat of the will (Acts 11:23), and it is that which determines moral conduct (Luke 16:15).

FLESH[12]

Only in the New Testament does the word "flesh" (Gk. *sarx*) take on a metaphorical or abstract meaning that corresponds to something in inner humanity. Nevertheless, the New Testament, especially Paul, probably has the basis for its abstract use in the Old Testament word for "flesh" (Heb. *basar*) because of the fact that the spiritual God is often contrasted with the fleshly person, giving rise to the idea in the New Testament that sin is somehow resident in the flesh.[13]

Paul uses *sarx* in three ways, besides the literal meaning: (1) humanity's creatureliness and frailty, which comes close to its Old Testament usage (Gal. 4:13); (2) that which is human, external, or natural (1 Cor. 1:26); and (3) a Pauline theological usage meaning that which is oriented toward the self, which pursues its own ends in self-seeking independence of God.

Elsewhere in the New Testament, "flesh," along with "blood," is sometimes contrasted with God (Matt. 16:17), and "fleshly desires" are seen as waging war against the soul (1 Pet. 2:11).

BODY[14]

As in the case of "flesh," many New Testament scholars believe that there is an abstract use of the Greek word *soma* to indicate the "whole person." Recently, however, this has been ably challenged by Robert Gundry, who believes that *soma* never means more than the physical body as the instrument of doing righteousness or doing sin.

Two prime passages are cited by those who believe in Paul's use as "whole person": Romans 6:12 and 12:1. Romans 6:12 is a command to present the body as an instrument of righteousness, not an instrument of sin, whereas Romans 12:1 likewise is a command to present our bodies as "living sacrifices" to God. Advocates of the "whole person" view, who frequently refer back to Rudolf Bultmann's *Theology of the New Testament* as their authority, see *soma* as Paul's "most comprehensive [term] for a human person."[15] Gundry would interpret the above passages as an appeal to present our physical bodies because they are the instruments through which we serve God.

Gundry examines the evidence from the Old Testament, classical Greek, the Septuagint, and other non-Pauline passages of the New Testament and concludes that the evidence for "whole person" is unconvincing. For example, in extrabiblical literature, slaves are often referred to as "bodies." The advocates of the "whole person" meaning interpret this as evidence of their view. Gundry believes that the explanation is that they were called "bodies" because of their common treatment as mere physical beings, a disparaging use of the term.[16]

In conclusion, since Paul had available to him other terms for the "whole person," or other ways in which to express that idea, I am inclined to reject the term *soma* as a reference to the inner being of humanity. Furthermore, the analogy of sacrifice behind Romans 6:12 and 12:1 strengthens the idea that a strictly physical concept of the body is in view. It was the body of the sacrifice in the Old Testament that was being offered, nothing more.

CONCLUSION

The rich vocabulary of the Old and New Testaments for the inner nature of humanity provides a superb vehicle for expressing the uniqueness of humanity as created in the image of God. Whether he had in mind the physical body or the inner being, the psalmist was truly accurate when he exclaimed, "I praise you because I am fearfully and wonderfully made" (Ps. 139:14).

For Further Thought

1. What corresponds and what differs between the biblical words for humanity's inner being and modern psychological concepts?

2. How has human depravity affected its inner being as revealed by the biblical terms?

For Further Reading

Elwell, Walter A., ed. *Evangelical Dictionary of Theology.* Grand Rapids: Baker, 1984. (The articles corresponding to the words treated in this chapter will serve as excellent summaries of this material and other theological implications.)

NOTES FOR CHAPTER 4

1. Material for this section has been largely gleaned from the following linguistic sources; abbreviations following each bibliographic reference will appear in subsequent footnotes to identify each work, along with the names of individual authors in the works, to conserve space: Colin Brown, ed., *The New International Dictionary of New Testament Theology*, 3 vols. (Grand Rapids: Zondervan, 1975)—NIDONTT; Geoffrey Bromiley, *Theological Dictionary of the New Testament*, abridged in one vol., Gerhard Kittel and Gerhard Friedrich, eds. (Grand Rapids: Eerdmans, 1985)—TDNT; R. Laird Harris, Gleason Archer, and Bruce K. Waltke, eds., *Theological Wordbook of the Old Testament*, 3 vols. (Chicago: Moody, 1980)—TWOT; Hans Walter Wolff, *Anthropology of the Old Testament* (Philadelphia: Fortress Press, 1974)—*Anthropology*.

2. Individual sources for "soul" are Bruce K. Waltke, TWOT, 2:587-91; Eduard Schweizer, TDNT, pp. 1347-51; Gunther Harder, NIDNTT, 3:676-86; Wolff, *Anthropology*, pp. 10-25.

3. Wolff notes this fact. He concludes that *nepesh* depicts humanity from the aspect of his need.

4. Individual sources for "spirit" are J. Barton Payne, TWOT, 1:836-37; Eduard Schweizer, TDNT, pp. 885-94; J. D. G. Dunn, NIDNTT, 3:693-707; Eberhard Kamlah, NIDNTT, 3:689-93; Wolff, *Anthropology*, pp. 32-39.

5. Gleason Archer, editorial note on the distinction between *ruah* and *nepesh* in TWOT, 1:837.

6. Wolff, *Anthropology*, pp. 32-39.

7. Individual sources for "mind" are E. Wurthwein, TDNT, p. 637; and Gunther Harder, NIDNTT, 3:122-30.

8. Individual sources for "conscience" are H. C. Hahn, NIDNTT, 1:348-51; and C. Maurer, TDNT, pp. 1120-24.

9. Hahn, NIDNTT, p. 350.

10. Individual sources for "heart" are Andrew Bowling, TWOT, 1:466-67; Theo Sorg, NIDNTT, 2:180-84; J. Behm, TDNT, p. 416; Wolff, *Anthropology*, pp. 40-58.

11. Wolff, *Anthropology*, pp. 40-58, categorizes *leb* as "reasonable man."

12. Individual sources for "flesh" are John N. Oswalt, TWOT, 1:136; Horst Seebass, NIDNTT, 1:671-78; Anthony Thiselton, NIDNTT, 1:678-82; Wolff, *Anthropology*, pp. 26-31; F. Baumgarten, TDNT, p. 1001; and Eduard Schweizer, TDNT, pp. 1003-7.

13. Wolff, *Anthropology*, pp. 26-31, interprets *basar* as humanity in its "infirmity."

14. Individual sources for "body" are Siegfried Wibbing, NIDNTT, 1:234-38; Eduard Schweizer, TDNT, pp. 1140-49; and Robert Gundry, *Soma in Biblical Theology with Emphasis on Pauline Anthropology* (Cambridge: Cambridge U., 1976).

15. Gundry, *Soma in Biblical Theology*, p. 6.
16. Ibid., p. 28.

5

HISTORY OF THE DOCTRINE
OF HUMANITY

Although the Bible has been considered the source of theology by orthodox believers from the very beginning, two factors have brought about a "development" of biblical truth so far as believers' perception of it is concerned.

One of these factors is the simple fact that the very profundity of the Bible has caused people to grow in their understanding of it. Some truth is obvious; or perhaps better, some elementary aspects of truth are obvious. But the longer one contemplates biblical truth, the greater the depth of his understanding.

The second of these factors is that misunderstanding of the truth of the Bible, both unintentional and deliberate, forces God's people to reexamine and clarify the truth. This involves the struggle against what has come to be known as "heresy." Each major biblical concept has witnessed such development, and the doctrine of humanity is no exception.

THE EARLY FATHERS

The early Fathers of the church were those leaders and writers who lived between the mid-first and mid-second centuries. Church historians have come to regard them as "Fathers" because of the early influence these men had on the development of the church and its teachings. The earliest of these men, known also as the apostolic Fathers, include Barnabas (who is probably not the Barnabas of Scripture but a pseudonym), Hermas, Clement of Rome, Polycarp, Papias, and Ignatius.

Several of these men had some things to say about the biblical teaching on anthropology. A striking difference is apparent to any reader who finishes the New Testament and moves into the apostolic Fathers. Depth and clarity are lacking in the apostolic Fathers, and their writings are simply inferior from a literary standpoint. Frankly, the greatest value of these Fathers is in their witness to the canonicity of books of the New Testament.

Generally speaking, the earliest Fathers were practical men more interested in everyday Christian living. There seems to be a tendency to see Christians capable of good works without reference to the work of the Holy Spirit. These Fathers are moralistic, issuing commands to their readers to do good works with the implication that this constitutes salvation. Few of these Fathers make reference to what later are cardinal points of the doctrine of humanity. For example, the *Epistle of Barnabas* (XII)[1] has the only reference among the apostolic Fathers to the fall of humanity, whereas Clement of Rome is the only one who refers to the fact that Adam was created in the image of God (*The First Epistle of Clement to the Romans*, XXXIII). There are early traces of what later became full-blown heresies. Polycarp, for instance, refutes the later Gnostic idea of the sinfulness of the human body, affirming that Jesus truly came "in the flesh" (The *Epistle to the Philippians*, VII). Overall, it can safely be said that when the apostolic Fathers refer to anthropology, they simply quote Scripture with little or no comment, leaving the obvious conclusion to their readers.

THE GROWING ANTITHESIS BETWEEN EAST AND WEST

During the second century of the Christian era a tendency began to develop that was to climax eventually in the great debate between Augustine and Pelagius. This debate would involve the question of the freedom of human will championed by Pelagius as opposed to the sovereignty of God defended by Augustine.

THE EASTERN FATHERS

The Fathers of the Eastern church tended to express views that would be expressed in more extreme form later by Pelagius in the debate between Pelagius and Augustine of Hippo.

Emphasis on the freedom of will can be found in Justin Martyr (100-165). In "Dialogue with Trypho" he says that "the human race . . . had fallen under the power of death and the guile of the serpent, . . . each one which had committed *personal* transgression" (*Dialogue with Trypho*, LXXXVIII [italics added]). In another place he affirms that the human race, "becoming like Adam and Eve, work out death *for themselves*" (*Dialogue*, CXXIV [italics added]). In other words, Justin Martyr sees no binding effect of the sin of Adam. Descendants of Adam seem merely to follow a pattern or influence set by him; there is no bondage of the will due to a sin nature inherited from Adam.

Clement of Alexandria (c. 155-220) sees humankind's rationality as the faculty capable of overcoming sin. In *The Stromata* (IV.3) he writes that "the soul is raised to God: trained in the true philosophy, it speeds to its kindred above, turning away from the lusts of the body, and besides these, from toil and fear, although we have shown that patience and fear belong to the good man."

In his *De Principiis*, Origen (c. 185-254) speaks of free will. He believes "that every rational soul is possessed of free-will and volition; that it has a struggle to maintain with the devil and his angels, and opposing influences, because they strive to burden it with sins" (Preface, 5). In his polemic *Against Celsus* (IV.40) Origen gives an interpretation of the Genesis account that sounds much like that of some modern neoorthodox interpreters: "In the Hebrew language Adam signifies man; and that in those parts of the narrative which appear to refer to Adam as an individual, Moses is discoursing upon the nature of man in general . . . not so much of *one particular individual* as of the *whole human race*" (italics added).

Athanasius's (298-373) greatest theological contribution was in his debate with Arius concerning the deity of Christ. Whenever he makes reference to the doctrine of humanity it is usually in connection with this other issue concerning Christ. Concerning depravity Athanasius is orthodox. In his discussion of the incarnation of Christ he says, "When transgression had once gained a start, men became involved in that corruption which was their nature, and were deprived of the grace which they had" (*Incarnation of the Word*, 7.4). Redeemed humanity is in a superior position to Adam, being "perfected in Him [Christ] and restored, as it was made at the beginning, nay, with greater grace" (*Against the Arians*, II, 67).

Athanasius may have been an early believer in the perfectibility of humanity in this life. At least some, according to him, could achieve this. For example, he declares that "many have been made holy and clean from all sin; nay Jeremiah was hallowed even from the womb [Jer. 1:5], and John, while yet in the womb, leapt for joy at the voice of Mary Bearer of God" (*Against the Arians*, II, 67).

Gregory (330-395) strangely believed that since procreation followed the Fall, both sexual differentiation and sexual intercourse result *from* the Fall. He says that "in a certain way the sin that entered into the world was profitable for the life of man: for the human race would have remained in the pair of the first-formed" (*On the Making of Man*, XVII). It was fear, he explains, that "impelled their nature to provide succession" (*Homilies on the Epistle to the Romans*, XVI). Gregory partly bases this idea on Jesus' teaching in Luke 20:35 about no marriage in heaven (*Homilies on Romans*, XVI).

Gregory also writes concerning the image of God:

> There is in us the principle of all excellence, all virtue and wisdom, and every higher thing that we conceive: but preeminent among all is the fact that we are free from necessity, and not in bondage to any natural power, but have decision in our own power as we please. . . . That which is the result of compulsion and force cannot be virtue. (*On the Making of Man*, XVI)

Thus to Gregory, freedom of will is an essential feature of the image of God.

John Chrysostom (c. 344-407) also emphasized the reality of human free will. In his homily on the epistle to the Romans he explains salvation strictly on the basis of human choice: "Now if all have sinned, how come some to be saved, and some to perish? It is because all were not minded to come to Him, since for His part all were saved, for all were called" (*Homilies on the Epistle to the Romans*, XVI). In the same homily he remarks on the reference to Esau and Jacob in Romans 9:11-13: "What was the cause then why one was loved and the other hated? . . . It was because one was wicked, and the other good."

Chrysostom has been accused of synergism (both humanity and God cooperate in humanity's doing good) on the basis of such a statement as is found in his homily on Hebrews:[2]

> What then? Does nothing depend on God? All indeed depends on God, but not so that our free-will is hindered. 'If

then it depend on God,' (one says), 'why does He blame us' On this account I said, 'so that our free-will is not hindered.' It depends then on us, and on Him. For we must first choose the good; and then He leads us to His own. He does not anticipate our choice, lest our free-will should be outraged. But when we have chosen, then great is the assistance he brings to us. (*Homilies on Hebrews*, XII)

John of Damascus (c. 675-749) is typical of the Eastern Fathers in his stress on free will and individual sinfulness. He affirms that "God makes all His works good, but each becomes of its own choice good or evil" (*Exposition of the Orthodox Faith*, II, xxi). John also believed in the distinction between image and likeness, the image being mind and free will and likeness pertaining to virtue (II, xii). He saw the person as a dichotomy in which "man's reason unites him to incorporeal and intelligent natures, for he applies his reason and mind and judgment to everything, and pursues after virtues, and eagerly follows after piety, which is the crown of the virtues. And so man is a microcosm" (II, xii).

THE WESTERN FATHERS

The Fathers of the Western church inclined in the direction that would culminate in the views of Augustine of Hippo. Though Irenaeus (185-195) believed in humanity's ability to make responsible choices because it retained the image of God, he considered humanity to be impaired in the sense that it lost the "likeness" of God, which he identified with God's holiness, something that would be restored at regeneration (*Against Heresies*, V.16.2). He also wrote that humanity was created in the image and likeness (or similitude) of God but at the Fall lost that likeness (V.6.1).

Known as the "father of western Christianity," Tertullian (c. 160-215) believed that sin was transmitted from Adam:

> Every soul, then, by reason of its birth, has its nature in
> Adam until it is born again in Christ; moreover, it is un-
> clean all the while that it remains without this regenera-
> tion; and because unclean, it is actively sinful, and suffuses
> even the flesh (by reason of their conjunction) with its own
> shame. (*On the Soul*, XL)

In another place he says that Adam, "having been consequently given over to death, made the whole race from that
time onward, infected from his seed, the bearer also of his
condemnation" (III). Humanity, however, is not without
any ability to do good, he says, for "there is a portion of
good in the soul, of that original, divine, and genuine good
which is its proper nature. For that which is derived from
God is rather obscured than extinguished" (XLI).

Thus, a person has a fully responsible free will in
"both tendencies [evil and good]; so that as master of himself, he might constantly encounter good by spontaneous
observance of it, and evil by its spontaneous avoidance"
(*Against Marcion*, VI). Only in this way can reward of either
good or evil be paid, because it is of choice and not necessity (XLI).

Tertullian was a dichotomist. Here is a sample of his
logic:

> Let the soul live without the spirit. . . . If indeed the soul
> and the spirit are two, they may be divided; and thus, by
> the separation of the one which departs from the one
> which remains, there would accrue the union and meeting
> together of life and of death. But such a union never will
> occur: therefore they are not two, and they cannot be divid-
> ed. (*On the Soul*, X)

Influenced by Stoic philosophy, Tertullian held to the
creationist view of the origin of the soul, which he says
sprang "from the breath of God." The soul is "immortal,
possessing body, having form, simple in its substance, in-

telligent in its own nature" (XXII). Both soul and body "are conceived, and formed, and perfected simultaneously, as well as born together" (XXVII). Since the soul has "body," it must be "sustained by meat and drink and after a time loses its vigour when they are withheld, and on their complete removal ultimately droops and dies" (XXXVII).

PELAGIUS VERSUS AUGUSTINE

The controversy over human ability to choose as opposed to God's sovereignty reached its climax in the debate between Augustine and Pelagius, a British monk in the fourth century of the Christian era. Simply stated, Augustine was a champion of the sovereignty of God whereas Pelagius was concerned that humanity recognize its absolute ability to make moral choices without any impairment by sin.

There are essentially two major categories into which the debate between these two men fall: the effects of the Fall of Adam on the human race as a whole, and the meaning of the grace of God.

THE EFFECT OF THE FALL ON THE HUMAN RACE

Pelagius (383-410) believed that it was possible for a person both to sin and not to sin. Nothing in his nature dictates either good or evil. In his *Pro Libero* Pelagius says:

> That man possesses this power of willing and effecting any good work comes from God alone [by creation he means]. . . . It is, therefore, at my own option not to have a good inclination and not to do a good action; but I am able not to have the possibility of good. This power is inherent in me whether I will or no.[3]

In another place he similarly says:

In our case, God himself . . . has sent us the holy Scriptures. . . . With hearts full of scorn and slackness, like proud and worthless servants, we shout in God's face and say, "It's hard! It's difficult! We can't!". . . We make the God of knowledge guilty of twofold ignorance: of not knowing what he has made, and of not knowing what he has commanded. . . . He has not willed to command anything impossible, for he is righteous; and he will not condemn a man for what he could not help, for he is holy.[4]

In the following quotation, Pelagius makes clear that the descendants of Adam are not affected by the Fall:

Everything good, and everything evil, on account of which we are either laudable or blameworthy, is not born with us but done by us: for we are born not fully developed, but with a capacity for either conduct; and we are procreated as without virtue, so also without vice; and previous to the action of our own proper will, that alone is in man which God has formed. (Quoted by Augustine in *On Original Sin*, 14)

In contrast to Pelagius, Augustine believed in the doctrine of original sin. Humanity was created without fault,

but that nature of man in which every one is born from Adam . . . is not sound. All good qualities, no doubt, which it still possessed in its make-up, life senses, intellect, it has of the Most High God. . . . But the flaw, which darkens and weakens all those natural goods, so that it has need of illumination and healing, it has not contracted from its blameless Creator—but from that original sin, which it committed by free will. (*On Nature and Grace*, 3)

Augustine's remarks on Romans 5:12 are clear:

For when the apostle says, "By one man sin entered the world, and death by sin, and so death passed upon all men," they will have it there understood not that "sin" passed over, but "death." What, then, is the meaning of what follows, "Wherein all have sinned"? For either the apostle says that in that "one man" all have sinned ... or else in that "sin," or certainly in "death."... Let them, then, choose which they will,—for either in that "man" all have sinned, ... or in that "sin" all have sinned, because that was the doing of all in general which all those who were born would have to derive. (*Against Two Letters of the Pelagians*, IV.7)

THE MEANING OF GRACE

Pelagius professed to believe in the grace of God, but to him it was a capacity in humanity granted by God at creation. Pelagius believed it possible for unregenerate humans not to sin, but God nevertheless should get the praise for this, "an acknowledgment of the power which we have received from him."[5] "No one," says Pelagius, "knows better the measure of our strength than he who gave us our strength."[6] Augustine quotes him in another place as saying that "the actual capacity of not sinning lies not so much in the power of will as in the necessity of nature. Whatever is placed in the necessity of nature undoubtedly appertains to the Author of nature, that is, God" (*On Nature and Grace*, 59).

Augustine, bishop of Hippo, understood grace as that which must be given by God directly. For believers God gives aid in the pursuit of righteousness through the "Holy Spirit, by whom there is formed in his mind a delight in, and love of, that supreme and unchangeable good which is God.... A man's free-will, indeed, avails for nothing except to sin, if he knows the way of truth (*On the Spirit and the Letter*, 5). For believers to persevere, they must be activated both in will and deed, "and they will just because *God works in them so to will* ... that [believers] might be unalterably irresistibly influenced by divine grace."[7]

CONCLUSION: THE COUNCIL OF CARTHAGE (A.D. 417)

The Council of Carthage ruled decisively against Pelagianism, but this decision was not widely popular in the church as a whole. Later, the Council of Arles (A.D. 473) condemned some of the conclusions of Augustinianism and advocated a semi-Pelagianism that held to human responsibility and the need for cooperation between human will and grace, but also affirmed an inherent disposition to sin. This doctrine became the prevailing view of the Roman church.

THE MIDDLE AGES

Generally speaking, the story of the period of time from about A.D. 500 to A.D. 1300, known as the Middle Ages, is the story of the tension between the views of Augustine of Hippo and Pelagius, i.e., the struggle between the role of divine grace as opposed to human effort and merit. This brief historical survey will deal only with the two most influential figures: Anselm of Canterbury and Thomas Aquinas.

Generally speaking, Anselm (1033-1109) followed Augustine. Concerning original sin, he says that since Adam and Eve

> committed personal sin . . . their whole being was weakened and corrupted. The body indeed, was weakened, because after sin it was just like the bodies of brute animals, subject to corruption and carnal desire. The soul, likewise, was weakened, because it was tainted by passions of the flesh. . . . And because the whole of human nature was in them . . . it was weakened and corrupted in its entirety.[8]

Anselm struggled with the question, Can original sin be imputed to infants? His conclusion was that the human race existed in Adam as a "nature" but not as individuals.

Although each person has at birth a sinful nature derived from his parents, he is not counted as a sinner unless he wills to act according to the bias of his nature. Anselm thus distinguished between "nature" and "person." In Adam, the person made nature sinful, and in birth the nature makes the person sinful.[9]

In the essay "On Freedom of Choice" Anselm expressed the idea that the ability to sin does not belong to freedom of choice, because then neither God nor angels who are not able to sin would have free choice.[10] Even after the Fall Adam still had free choice. There was no compulsion to sin, but he sinned through his own choice, by the ability he had to sin.[11]

In Thomas Aquinas (1225-1274) there is a blending of Augustinianism and semi-Pelagianism. Humanity, he says, is able to do righteousness by the addition of a kind of grace in its creation (*Summa Theologica*, I, Q83, 1).[12] Humanity has free will, but it must be "moved and helped by God" (I, Q83, 1).

Aquinas's ability to systematize and make a fine, judicial point was unexcelled, and nowhere else did it find a finer expression than in his view of how sin could come to exist in a created being such as Adam in whom there was no inherent flaw. He explains it in terms of Adam's knowledge of God. This knowledge was a knowing *about* God. To have *known* God would have been to have *loved* God and hence never to have sinned. "Wherefore no one who sees the Essence of God can willingly turn away from God, which means to sin" (I, Q94, 1).

Aquinas was opposed to the Traducian idea of the origin of all souls in Adam, because, as he put it, "all men born of Adam may be considered as one man, inasmuch as they have one common nature, which they receive from their first parents" (I, Q81, 1).

Nevertheless, as to original sin, Aquinas was Augustinian. Children are baptized, he explained, because the sin of Adam was transmitted to his descendants, and "they have to be washed from some uncleanness." The contrary, he observes, is part of the Pelagian heresy (II, Q81, 1).

Finally, Aquinas is known for his doctrine of "habitual" grace as distinct from "actual" grace. He explained it in the following way:

> In order to live righteously a man needs a two-fold help of God—first, a habitual gift whereby corrupted human nature is healed, and after being healed is lifted up so as to work deeds meritorious of everlasting life, which exceed the capability of nature. Secondly, man needs the help of grace in order to be moved by God to act. (II, Q109, 9)

CONCLUSION

The Middle Ages are by modern standards a dull time theologically. Little advance was made, and perhaps considerable ground was lost as theologians became preoccupied with trivial issues such as "whether separated souls know what takes place on earth" (*Summa Theologica*, I, Q89, 8). The world was ready for the Reformation.

THE REFORMATION

The revival of biblical exegesis resulting from the renewed exchange of learning with the East had to have its effect eventually. John Wycliffe, sometimes called the "morning star of the Reformation," was impelled by his new understanding of the Scriptures and began a trend that would be continued by those we think of as the "Reformers." So far as the doctrine of humanity is concerned, the days of the Reformation were days of dispute over whether or not free will exists.

In his classic *The Bondage of the Will*, Luther (1483-1546) interprets such passages as Romans 1:18ff; 3:9ff; and 3:21ff as disproving the existence of free will. For example, on Romans 3:9, he states,

Where is "free-will" now? All Jews and Greeks, he says, are under sin. Are there any "figures" or "knots" here? What can the whole world's "explanation" avail against this perfectly clear statement? By saying "all" he excepts none. By describing them all as "under sin," that is, slaves of sin, he leaves them no goodness.[13]

Similarly, Luther comments on Romans 3:21-26: "And though I should grant that 'free-will' by its endeavours can advance in some direction, namely, in the direction of good works, or the righteousness of the civil or moral law, yet it does not advance towards God's righteousness."[14]

Phillip Melanchthon (1497-1650), a follower of Luther, generally expressed himself in about the same way, except in the case of justification by grace. Afraid that some might interpret the concept of free grace as license to sin (antinomianism), his influence can be detected in the Augsburg confession (1530), Article VI: "Also they teach that this faith should bring forth good fruits, and that men ought to do the good works commanded of God, because it is God's will, and not on any confidence of meriting justification before God by their works."[15] Thus Melanchthon modified Luther's stricter view of total inability and allowed for some ability, at least by regenerated people, to will to do good. In this respect, he has had a greater influence on later Lutherans than Luther himself.

Yet Melanchthon was a true advocate of justification by grace alone. In his "Loci Communes Theologici" he criticized the followers of Thomas Aquinas "who have placed the quality of 'grace' in the nature of the soul, and faith, hope, and love in the powers of the soul. How old-womanish and stupid is the way they dispute about powers of the soul!"[16]

Ulrich Zwingli (1484-1531) is significant in contrast to Melanchthon in his stricter view against free will and serves as the opposite fork in the road in his influence of later generations. Zwingli went so far as to advocate arbitrary omnipotence of God, sometimes also known as "double" predestination of both good and evil. Human beings, he taught, are instigated by God to sin,

> but for this purpose, that the one should be translated, the other nailed to the cross. Here the champions of free-will, the logical opponents of Providence, are under a delusion. [Providence] not only influences and impels men until murder takes place, but goes further, and forces the judge by the law which goads him with the sting of conscience, drives him by the example of cruelty to bind the robber and raises him upon the cross.[17]

John Calvin (1509-1564) continued the trend established by Zwingli, that depravity, if taken seriously, implies the enslavement of the human will. In Book II of the *Institutes* Calvin rebuts the current speculative and biblical arguments for free will by concluding that grace is absolutely necessary and total and that predestination is absolute.[18] Calvin followed Augustine in agreeing that the human race is sinful on account of Adam, but he rejected the idea of a sinful nature propagated by natural generation:

> For the contagion does not take its origin from the substance of the flesh or soul, but because it had been so ordained by God that the first man should at one and the same time have and lose, both for himself and for his descendants, the gifts that God had bestowed upon him.[19]

THE COUNCIL OF TRENT

The Roman Catholic church responded at the Council of Trent (1537-1563) against the monergism (only grace can save) of the Protestant Reformation with a dogmatic formulation of semi-Pelagian synergism (humanity must cooperate with divine grace). The most significant items so far as anthropology is concerned are what the Roman Catholic divines had to say about free will and original sin.

One canon states, "If anyone says that after the sin of Adam man's free will was lost and destroyed, . . . let him be anathema."[20] Concerning Adam's sin, another canon declares, "If anyone asserts that the transgression of Adam injured himself alone, and not his posterity . . . or that he . . . has only transfused death and pains of the body into the whole human race, let him be anathema."[21]

ARMINIANISM

So far as the doctrine of anthropology is concerned, the debate of the Reformers over whether humanity has free will or not became part of a larger debate between Calvinism and Arminianism. In our brief examination, however, we will look only at the differences on the issue of the effects of the Fall on human ability to do good. James Arminius reflected the sentiments of those who took issue with some of Calvin's views on humanity's depravity as well, of course, as Calvin's views on predestination and irresistible grace.

Generally speaking, strict Calvinism holds to the tenet that humanity is totally unable to will to do good. In fact, this applies even to Christians who are regenerated; in their case the Holy Spirit must both energize the will as well as enable the believer after he wills to obey God. Contrary to this, the Arminian believes in free will even on the part of the unregenerated, though the Fall has resulted in a sort of inclination toward sin. This inclination can be overcome by prevenient grace given to all. It is by divine grace.[22]

As to Adam's sin, Arminius believed that a distinction must be made between "actual" sin and that which *causes* sin. Adam's first sin was not a common act of humanity, and evil tendencies themselves are not a source of condemnation. Sin must be "voluntary" before it can condemn.[23] He explains Adam's sin as follows:

> When Adam sinned in his own person and with his free will, God pardoned that transgression. There is no reason then why it was the will of God to impute this sin to infants, who are said to have sinned in Adam, before they had any personal existence, and therefore before they could possibly sin at their own will and pleasure.[24]

John Wesley (1703-1791) perhaps gave the greatest popular impetus to Arminian theology through his preaching. In his writings on original sin he replies to the question, Do we not have from Adam a moral taint and infection, whereby we have a natural propensity to sin? Wesley answers, "They have all . . . a natural propensity to sin. Nevertheless, this propensity is not necessary, if by necessary you mean irresistible. We can resist and conquer it too by the grace which is ever at hand."[25]

CLASSIC LIBERALISM

Liberalism or "modernism" is essentially a revival of ancient Pelagianism so far as biblical anthropology is concerned. The theory of evolution is applied to theology, and thus the effects of the Fall are either minimized or totally disregarded. Humanity is not depraved in either the Calvinistic or Arminian sense of the term.

Friedrich Schleiermacher is often called the "father" of modern liberalism. Schleiermacher believed that theology should go beyond the Bible and include every aspect of human experience as its source of truth. Original sin, according to Schleiermacher, is "the sinfulness that is present in an individual prior to any action of his own."[26] So far as the sin of Adam is concerned, he says, "we have no reason for explaining universal sinfulness as due to an alteration in human nature brought about in their person by the first sin."[27] Instead, "universal sinfulness ... is to be regarded not so much as derived from the first sin of our first parents, but rather as identical with what in them likewise preceded the first sin, so that in committing their first sin they were simply the first-born of sinfulness."[28]

What, then, is this that "preceded" the first sin? Some believe that Schleiermacher is thinking of the "brute" in humanity from its more primitive state, not exactly an evolutionary idea, since Darwin had not yet proposed his theory. He sees it as a conflict between this primal force and "God-consciousness," which has not yet fully emerged.[29]

Schleiermacher, nevertheless, remained somewhat of a confessionalist toward orthodox Christian doctrine, in spite of departures such as this. Only redemption by Christ can restore humanity. Original sin is "the personal guilt of every individual," and the recognition of it as such is likewise recognition of the universal need of redemption.[30]

Another early "liberal" was Albrecht Ritschl (1822-1889). The basic assumption of his primary theological work, *The Christian Doctrine of Justification and Reconciliation*, is that Christianity should be divorced from its alliance with philosophy, as had been the case since the days of the early Fathers. Though this may have a natural appeal to many modern evangelicals, it did not mean that the Bible would be restored to its role as primary source for theology. Like Schleiermacher, Ritschl resorted to human reason and experience as equally important authorities.

In the fifth chapter of his work, Ritschl sets forth his doctrine of sin. He explains sin as "opposition to good" that arises through the influences of our environment, or, as he called it, the "kingdom of sin," which is opposed to the kingdom of God: "We also feel the reaction of this power of common sin, not only through example or the production in us of sinful opposition to the sins of others, but especially by the blunting of our moral vigilance and our moral judgment.[31]

Ritschl, further, does not define sin as a moral offense against God nor does he believe that it incurs the retribution of God. These ideas, he maintains, result from the mistaken idea that sin and law-breaking in relation to God must be seen the same way lawlessness is dealt with in the civil or human realm. This concept of God is wrong. In fact, to punish Adam and Eve for their transgression on the basis of some supposed standard of justice would have gone contrary to God's purpose in creating them.[32] Finally, Ritschl contends, sin is more a matter of *ignorance* than anything else, which, "experience teaches in the case of children, is a very significant factor in the origin and development of sin."[33]

The rise of modern liberalism was aided and abetted by the advent of Charles Darwin's *Origin of Species* in 1859. Although Darwin postulated a theory of biological history, it was natural that the same principle be applied to human theological history as well. Ordinary evolution accounts for human origin solely by chance, not by a Creator. Humanity has not devolved, but evolved. Classical liberalism, however, saw this otherwise materialistic concept in more theistic terms: God was at the beginning of evolution and involved in its processes. At some point God placed what the Bible calls the image of God into the first human, mythically portrayed by the Genesis story of Adam and Eve.

Another influential factor in classical liberalism was the influence of Sigmund Freud (1856-1939). Freud's obsession was what he called "neurosis"—what causes it and how it can be cured. But Freud went beyond mere psychoanalysis and suggested that religion itself was a neurosis. To Freud the essence of human personality was the unconscious, and this part of humanity is largely motivated by the sex drive. Modern liberalism was, in spite of Freud's antireligious assumptions, highly influenced by his analysis of human behavior, and this was incorporated in its counseling methodology. To do this, of course, meant to ignore the values of biblical assumptions, especially those pertaining to human sinfulness.

H. D. McDonald has aptly summed up these two influences:

> If Darwin is right, then man is no more than a blown-up ape; or, if Freud is right, then man is not other than a sex-obsessed biped. Actually neither Darwin nor Freud is right, because neither takes full account of all the data of man's nature. Man is not accounted for in terms of mere animality; nor yet in terms of mere sexuality. It follows, therefore, that his salvation does not consist in curbing a few unruly brutish instincts; nor in sublimination of the one lustful instinct.[34]

THE NEOORTHODOX RESPONSE TO LIBERALISM

Liberalism had bought in to evolutionary humanism to the extent that the biblical ideas of Adam's fall into sin and his depravity (balanced by Adam's creation in the image of God) were laid aside. Due to the reactions of two men, Karl Barth (1886-1968) and Emil Brunner (1889-1966), an attempt to return to orthodoxy took place. This "new orthodoxy," as it came to be known, once again stressed the revelation of God and the fallenness of man.

Unique to Barth's and Brunner's view of humanity was a departure from the classic formulations of the image of God usually based on something intrinsic within: the "image" was a person's ability to relate to God.[35] This was the outcome of the dominating philosophy of the day—existentialism—which tended to root the search for truth in humanity's experience. (Even the Bible, according to Barth and Brunner, was "revelation" only in the sense that it recorded the experience that a person had of a divine revelational encounter with God.)

CONCLUSION

Throughout history, the storm centers of debate about what humanity is have been the questions of how we explain sin and to what extent freedom of will exists. Today these questions are answered variously among evangelical Christians, whether they follow the more Calvinistic idea of total depravity or the Arminian ideas of partial depravity or prevenient grace.

The ideas of neoorthodoxy and classic liberalism tend to show up in nonevangelical theologies as some sort of blend. So far as anthropology is concerned, there is little that is radically new today.

But one's view of anthropology radically affects the rest of his theology, especially whether or not he is involved in evangelism. If humanity is not depraved, evangelism is not needed; instead, further education is required. If humanity is not depraved, grace is not needed to save it.

FOR FURTHER THOUGHT

1. Why is the issue of humanity's freedom or lack of it such an important matter for debate through the centuries?

2. What bearing does one's view of human depravity have on this?

FOR FURTHER READING

H. D. MacDonald, "Doctrine of Man." In *Evangelical Dictionary of Theology*, ed. Walter Elwell, pp. 878-80. Grand Rapids: Baker, 1984. (MacDonald offers a brief summary of major issues throughout Christian history.)

NOTES FOR CHAPTER 5

1. References to the early Fathers, both those who preceded the Council of Nicea as well as those during and after, unless otherwise noted, are taken from *The Ante-Nicene Fathers*, ed. Alexander Roberts and James Donaldson (Grand Rapids: Eerdmans, 1969); and *Nicene and Post-Nicene Fathers*, 2d series, ed. Philip Schaff and Henry Wace (Grand Rapids: Eerdmans, 1961). All such documentation, therefore, will be placed within the text.

2. Thus H. D. McDonald, *The Christian View of Man* (Westchester, Ill.: Crossway, 1981), p. 56.

3. "Pro Libero Arbitrio," in *The Anti-Pelagian Works of St. Augustine*, 2: 5f. The text is that appearing in J. Stevenson, ed., *Creeds, Councils and Controversies: Documents Illustrative of the History of the Church* A.D. 337-461 (London: SPCK, 1966), pp. 217-18.

4. "Letter to Demetrius," 16. Ibid., p. 219.

5. "Pro Libero Arbitrio," 2:5f. Ibid., pp. 217-18.

6. "Letter to Demetrius," 16. Ibid., p. 219.

7. "Of Corruption and Grace," 38, in *Documents of the Christian Church*, 2d ed., ed. Henry Bettenson (Oxford: Oxford U., 1970), p. 78.

8. Anselm of Canterbury, *The Virgin Conception and Original Sin*, trans. Joseph M. Colleran, chap. 2 (Albany, N.Y.: Magi Books, 1969), p. 171.

9. Ibid., chaps. 7, 12, 22.

10. Anselm, "On Freedom of Choice," in *Truth, Freedom, and Evil: Three Philosophical Dialogues*, ed. and trans. Jasper Hopkins and Herbert Richardson, chap. 1, (N.Y.: Harper Torchbooks, 1965, 1967), p. 122.

11. Ibid., chap. 3, p. 124.

12. Thomas Aquinas, *Summa Theologica* (New York: Benziger Brothers, 1947). All subsequent quotations of Thomas will be from this work and placed in the text.

13. Martin Luther, *The Bondage of the Will*, trans. J. I. Packer and O. R. Johnson (Westwood, N.J.: Revell, 1957), p. 278.

14. Ibid., p. 289.

15. Philip Schaff, *The Creeds of Christendom* (Grand Rapids: Baker, 1977), 3:11.

16. William Pauck, ed., *Melanchthon and Bucer*, vol. 19 of *The Library of Christian Classics* (Philadelphia: Westminster, 1969), p. 87.

17. Ulrich Zwingli, *On Providence and Other Essays*, ed. William John Hinke (Durham, N.C.: Labyrinth, 1922), p. 183.

18. John Calvin, *Institutes of the Christian Religion* II, 5, 16-19, ed. John T. McNeill, trans. Ford Lewis Battles (Philadelphia: Westminster, 1960), 1:123-40.

19. *Institutes* 11, 1, 7, 1:250.

20. *Canons and Decrees of the Council of Trent*, trans. H. J. Schroeder (London: Herder, 1941), p. 43.

21. Ibid., pp. 21-22.

22. James Arminius, "Twenty-five Public Disputations," XI, in *The Works of James Arminius*, trans. James and William Nichols (Grand Rapids: Baker, 1986), 2:192.

23. James Arminius, "Apology," XXXI, 2:60.

24. "Apology," II, 2:11-12.

25. John Wesley, "Original Sin," II, in *The Works of John Wesley* (Grand Rapids: Baker, 1978), 9:294.

26. Friedrich Schleiermacher, *The Christian Faith*, ed. H. R. Mackintosh and J. S. Stewart (Edinburgh: T. and T. Clark, 1928), p. 282.

27. Ibid., p. 291.

28. Ibid., p. 299.

29. Ibid., p. 273.

30. Ibid., p. 285.

31. Albrecht Ritschl, *The Christian Doctrine of Justification and Reconciliation*, trans. H. R. Mackintosh and A. B. Macaulay (Edinburgh: T. and T. Clark, 1900), p. 338.

32. Ibid., p. 256.

33. Ibid., p. 377.

34. H. D. McDonald, *The Christian View of Man*, p. 113.

35. Emil Brunner, *Man in Revolt* (Philadelphia: Westminster, 1948), pp. 102-5; Karl Barth, *Church Dogmatics*, trans. Geoffrey Bromiley (Edinburgh: T. and T. Clark, 1956-60), 3:184, 214.

6

SOME IMPLICATIONS OF BIBLICAL ANTHROPOLOGY

An understanding of the biblical doctrine of humanity affects several areas of modern thought and activity quite profoundly. One of the foibles of modern evangelical Christianity is its failure to integrate biblical truth with current human thought and theory. Instead, Christians today tend to accept modern thought rather uncritically and thus entertain conflicting ideas without realizing it.

In chapter 1 we interacted with one such implication in regard to modern scientific theories of human origins. There remain three other areas that demand attention, however: psychology, sociology, and evangelism. Modern psychology is characterized by numerous theories about the nature of humanity that conflict with the biblical picture; racism is a societal evil that needs to be evaluated in light of biblical anthropology; and modern evangelism needs to come under the scrutiny of the biblical teaching on man's nature.

BIBLICAL ANTHROPOLOGY VS. PSYCHOLOGY'S HUMANISM

Psychology and biblical Christianity have been at odds with each other almost from the beginning of psychology as a science. Some of the tension has resulted from overreaction on the part of some Christians who were inclined to reject psychology and psychiatry as a whole because of certain obviously antibiblical biases on the part of these sciences. When psychology goes beyond mere observation and analysis of data and moves into theory, its antibiblical presumptions begin to show up, and that is where the antagonism has occurred.

Among Bible-believing Christians there has arisen a movement that has attempted to integrate biblical principles with psychology and psychiatry, but even within this group there are wide differences of opinion as to how much of modern psychology is usable without contradicting biblical truth. It is beyond the scope of this textbook to investigate this controversy, but we can identify those basic truths of the biblical view of humanity that all Christians agree conflict with assumptions of modern humanistic psychology.

But before we look at those truths, we need to define "humanism," because that is the characteristic of most modern forms of psychology and psychiatry that concerns us. *Webster's New Collegiate Dictionary* defines it as "a philosophy that asserts the dignity and worth of man and his capacity for self-realization through reason and that often rejects supernaturalism." The Bible, of course, teaches the dignity and worth of man, but the part of the definition that introduces the antibiblical elements begins with the word "reason" and ends with the words "rejects supernaturalism."

The Bible supports belief in reason, but reason without God (made clear by the words "rejects supernaturalism") ultimately turns into atheism. Note Paul's words in 1 Corinthians 1:18-21:

> For the message of the cross is foolishness to those who are perishing, but to us who are being saved it is the power of God. For it is written: "I will destroy the wisdom of the wise; the intelligence of the intelligent I will frustrate."

Where is the wise man? Where is the scholar? Where is the philosopher of this age? Has not God made foolish the wisdom of the world? For since in the wisdom of God the world through its wisdom did not know him, God was pleased through the foolishness of preaching to save those who believe.

Man's unaided reason does not lead him to God. The fundamental factor in humanism that affects all its conclusions is that it simply leaves God out of its thinking and investigation. Let us note those fundamental truths about the biblical view of humanity that conflict with humanistic psychology.

HUMANITY IS CREATED IN THE IMAGE OF GOD

Most modern humanistic psychology assumes the great worth and uniqueness of humanity, but it is not a well-grounded assumption. Generally, psychologists assume that the uniqueness of humanity is due to its ability to reason but little more. In other words, people are merely rational animals, higher than the animal kingdom because they can think and reflect about themselves. Such thinking is rooted in the theory of evolution. One psychology text, for example, has this to say:

> After the great biologist Charles Darwin published his theory of evolution in *On the Origin of the Species* in 1859, people's conception of themselves underwent a fundamental change. No longer was a human a unique creature, completely different from the animals; instead, he was part of the animal kingdom—a species that had evolved by natural selection in the same way that all other animal species had evolved. To be sure, humans were unique in some ways, but at the same time they were similar in many ways to other species, especially apes and other primates. By placing humans firmly within the animal kingdom, Darwin laid the foundation for the field of psychology. In fact, publica-

tion of *On the Origin of the Species* is regarded by some people as marking the beginning of psychology as a legitimate field.[1]

The biblical concept of humanity created in the image of God contrasts radically with this. First of all, the Bible declares by this concept that a human is indeed a creature, not God. One of the curious results of evolutionary humanism is that humanity itself becomes a kind of "god." Being the product of totally natural processes, it has no higher being to whom it must answer. Thus, a sort of deification takes place, and humanity is the master of its own destiny.

Second, the concept of the image of God makes humanity totally unique above the animal creation. Psychology elevates humanity to a superior position over the animal but without adequate reason, except that humans can think in a superior way. The biblical view of humanity gives people dignity that derives from the Creator Himself, so that it includes more than mere rationality. (See chap. 2 for what this includes.)

Third, the concept of the image of God gives humanity inestimable worth. Psychologists are able to examine a person and recognize worth because of the complexity of his physical and rational being, but in the final analysis they can claim that he is merely of greater worth because he is a more developed animal. Marxist societies are more consistent than evolutionists in their view of the relative value of human life because they are able to justify the purge of certain human beings for the greater good of society, whereas most evolutionists do not condone such a practice.

HUMANITY IS FUNDAMENTALLY CORRUPTED BY SIN

Psychologists observe human behavior and acknowledge that human beings are selfish and self-centered and often characterized by unacceptable behavior, but their ideas on why and what to do about it differ radically from the Bible.

If the human being is an evolving animal, as psychologists believe, then he will overcome lower brute characteristics, given enough time. Some psychologists believe that people's behavior can be changed through careful training and psychoanalysis. The answers to unacceptable human behavior are, therefore, education and behavior modification.

Though Sigmund Freud advocated theories not widely accepted anymore by most psychologists, he nevertheless is characteristic in the way he explains sin and guilt. For example, Freud theorized that human guilt and conscience originated from ancient taboos, not the violation of divine law. Freud defined "taboo" as something sacred and unapproachable. When a taboo was violated remorse was felt and thus conscience originated. Taboo restrictions, Freud speculated, are distinct from religious or moral prohibitions; they "impose themselves on their own account."[2]

The Bible, of course, teaches that God originates laws, people break those laws starting with Adam, the first human, and therefore guilt results. As a matter of fact, humanity has been so radically affected by the first Fall that it is basically inclined to break God's laws again and again. Fundamentally sin is hostility toward and rebellion against God; even the good that a person does is not done in loving obedience to God but for some selfish reason.

Furthermore, the Bible teaches that the remedy for bad behavior is a radical inward transformation within a person through regeneration; a basic revolution of inner motives and desires. People cannot otherwise be reprogrammed. Counseling and training can help to control rebellious human nature and can contribute to the growth in holiness of regenerated people, but they cannot accomplish anything lasting or fundamental by themselves.

HUMANITY IS ULTIMATELY RESPONSIBLE FOR ITS DECISIONS

B. F. Skinner's influence has been widespread. In his landmark book *Beyond Freedom and Dignity*, he challenges the notion of human freedom. (See chap. 2 and the discussion of human freedom.) Skinner believes that all behavior is conditioned by genetic and environmental influences. One of the outcomes of his view is that people are not responsible for their acts; therefore, punishment does not necessarily alter behavior. Skinner says, "It is the environment which is 'responsible' for the objectionable behavior, and it is the environment, not some attribute of the individual, which must be changed."[3]

Such a view as this has filtered down into the criminal justice system and is also a major influence in education, but some psychiatrists such as Hobart Mowrer[4] and Karl Menninger[5] have reacted against it. Such a view is clearly contrary to the biblical teaching about humanity. We discussed the various views among Christian theologians on the nature of human freedom in chapter 2, but regardless of their differences, all maintained that human beings created in the image of God are responsible for their acts.

The answer to guilt according to Scripture is to acknowledge it and seek God's forgiveness, i. e., to accept responsibility. Sin is real, not an illusion to be explained away. Psychiatrist Hobart Mowrer recognizes this fact:

> Recovery ... is most assuredly attained, not by helping a person reject and rise above his sins, but by helping him accept them. ... He cannot (if he has any character at all) "accept himself"; and all our efforts to reassure and accept him will avail nothing. ... But the moment he (with or without "assistance") begins to accept his guilt and his sinfulness, the possibility of radical reformation opens up.[6]

BIBLICAL ANTHROPOLOGY VERSUS RACISM AND PREJUDICE

Sin is not only an individual thing; it affects society in various ways. Evangelical Christianity has also been negligent in recognizing and dealing with societal evil in its emphasis on personal salvation. A biblical understanding of humanity provides the best explanation and cure of societal sins.

Millard Erickson is correct when he says, "We may become quite sensitized to God's displeasure with our individual sins, but be considerably less aware of the sinfulness of a group of which we are part."[7] Examples of societal sin are numerous: the lack of justification for a particular war our nation undertakes; the tendency to oppress certain groups or the poor within a society; nationalistic or clannish pride that blinds us to injustices done in the name of patriotism or fidelity to the group.

There is a form of social sin to which biblical anthropology most directly speaks: racism and ethnic prejudice. Racism is the belief on the part of one race that it is superior to another or that some race is inferior to all the rest. Ethnic prejudice is of the same species, except that it is directed against a different culture or nationality. Sometimes the two blend together when both race and culture are involved. Racism and ethnic prejudice result in the outward evils of segregation and discrimination, but inwardly they involve an attitude toward a person or group that is unfounded in light of the biblical revelation concerning humanity. There is no ground in reality for any kind of prejudice, whether racial or ethnic, once a few basic biblical truths about humanity are brought into focus.

HUMANITY'S COMMON ORIGIN

The first biblical truth pertinent to racism or prejudice is that all human beings have a common ancestor—

Adam. When dealing with the snobbish Athenians, the apostle Paul put it this way:

> The God who made the world and everything in it . . . gives all men life and breath and everything else. From one man he made every nation of men, that they should inhabit the whole earth; and he determined the times set for them and the exact places where they should live. (Acts 17:24-26)

What that means, of course, is that all humanity had the same start. No alleged deficiencies among races or nationalities can be laid at the door of origins as described in the Bible. Although evolutionists may not be in agreement as to how human evolution began, whether from a common ancestor or from several independent beginnings, the biblical teaching is that Adam is a common ancestor, and this lays to rest any claim of superiority due to some natural variation in evolution, at least as far as the Bible-believer is concerned.

HUMANITY'S COMMON SIN

According to Romans 5, original sin has affected the entire human race equally. It is true that depravity, so far as behavior is concerned, occurs in varying degrees from one individual to another, but alienation toward God is equal among all human beings. Since this kind of depravity is the ultimate cause of all evil in the human race, no group or race can be alleged to have a corner on sin or bad characteristics.

THE POTENTIAL FOR REDEMPTION

The Bible does recognize that some ethnic groups have developed bad characteristics, but this is not a contradiction of what I have said above. To explain this, observe the advice of Paul to Titus concerning the Cretans:

For there are many rebellious people, mere talkers and deceivers, especially those of the circumcision group. They must be silenced, because they are ruining whole households by teaching things they ought not to teach—and that for the sake of dishonest gain. Even one of their own prophets has said, "Cretans are always liars, evil brutes, lazy gluttons." This testimony is true. Therefore, rebuke them sharply so that they will be sound in the faith and will pay no attention to Jewish myths or to the commands of those who reject the truth. (Titus 1:10-14)

At first glance, Paul may appear to be prejudiced, but if you consider his advice on how to deal with the situation you will realize that he is not prejudiced but *realistic*—realistic concerning the form depravity takes in certain groups—and hopeful that this sin can be remedied. This is not racism, for racists reject people to whom they feel superior; they do not offer constructive advice on how to correct unacceptable behavior.

Notice also that Paul is advising Titus concerning those within the church. He has hope because these people are probably regenerated, the best possible basis for lasting change. Unfortunately, when change occurs among unregenerated people, such change often leads to self-righteousness, which only perpetuates prejudice.

A racist often overlooks his own faults. Either he does the same things in another form that he criticizes in a different group or he has another kind of fault of his own. (A parallel to this is described by Paul in Rom. 2:1-4.) In the Southern state where I was raised, it was common for whites to criticize poor blacks for their run-down neighborhoods, but I remember vividly people the wealthier whites called "poor white trash" who lived in hovels underneath bridges in far greater squalor that most blacks.

THE REAL CAUSE OF RACISM AND PREJUDICE

The real cause of racism and prejudice lies in the sin nature, not in the environment. Bad environments are ultimately due to original sin. Most modern sociologists readily indict particular societies as seedbeds of racism, but this reflects the influence of such men as B. F. Skinner. No one is without the tendency toward racism, thus the most enlightened and tolerant society would still have the elements of prejudice somewhere in it. Even Christians harbor prejudices in their congregations. Paul noted that such a situation was at least potentially present at the Asia Minor city of Colossae:

> Do not lie to each other, since you have taken off your old self with its practices and have put on the new self, which is being renewed in knowledge in the image of its Creator. Here there is no Greek or Jew, circumcised or uncircumcised, barbarian, Scythian, slave or free, but Christ is all, and is in all. (Col. 3:9-11)

The words "old self" are a Pauline term for the depraved way of life they used to live, whose tendencies still remain in Christian believers. The close contextual connection with "old self" and the statement that differences between them, such as Jew and Gentile, barbarian and Scythian—things that give rise to prejudice—show that the origin of prejudice is in the sin nature and that former distinctions should not continue to prevail in the redeemed community.

BIBLICAL ANTHROPOLOGY AND ITS EFFECT ON EVANGELISM

It is often an irony of modern evangelicalism that evangelism is attempted without careful correlation with what the Bible says about human nature. That is incredible, because evangelism should be the answer to the human condition, but if you do not understand the human condition, you cannot really evangelize.

THE IMPLICATION OF THE IMAGE OF GOD

Besides the fact that Christians are commanded to evangelize, there is another motivating factor often overlooked in evangelism that would stimulate desire and compassion: the great worth and potential of human beings, which only redemption can fully bring out.

Prejudice and revulsion toward unpleasant traits in people frequently stifle the outgoing spirit that needs to characterize good evangelism. The most outwardly depraved and disgusting individual must be seen in light of what he might become through regeneration and sanctification to overcome this prejudice and revulsion. The image of God is marred in the best of us and so distorted that it is easy to consider a person as beyond hope. But all humans are created in the image of God. Some indeed will never respond, but the effort is always worth it.

THE IMPLICATION OF HUMAN DEPRAVITY

There is really no need for evangelism if a person is not totally depraved. Instead, reformation and education would be the answers. But reformation and education are not making this a better world. Redemption is the only way to change society in a lasting way. The change can occur without everyone's being regenerated, but it cannot occur without some being regenerated.

Several aspects of human depravity come to bear upon evangelism. First of all, the fact of human depravity makes clear that the evangelist is dependent on the work of the Holy Spirit. John says that when the Holy Spirit comes "he will convict the world of guilt in regard to sin and righteousness and judgment." Anyone who has faced the obstinate unbelief of someone as he spoke to him about the gospel knows how futile it is to try to convince him of his need for Christ, and if a person happens to be receptive, this itself is the result of the Spirit's work in advance.

Second, it is also obvious that the only remedy for a person's alienation from God is the truth that God's righteousness is available to him by faith alone. But this faith requires repentance of sin—acknowledgment that one is indeed a sinner—before it is possible to appropriate the righteousness of God by faith. Thus, the gospel must be presented in such a way that the human condition is clearly spelled out. This will inevitably anger some and often bring about some form of persecution. The evangelist must be prepared to tell the truth regardless of this.

Therefore, an accurate gospel message must include such things as the justice and holiness of God, the reason for humanity's present condition, and exactly what sin is beyond mere acts of sin; namely, that sin arises out of a sinful tendency with which all humans are born. It must be presented with the understanding that righteousness by faith leads to righteousness in behavior, not merely forgiveness. This is not to require some effort on the sinner's part alone but God-empowered obedience to Scripture, a work of God's grace within the person's life.

FOR FURTHER THOUGHT

1. What would be wrong with telling a person who feels guilty about his lack of responsibility that he is that way because his parents never taught him to be responsible?

2. What deficiencies in counseling would exist with a skilled psychiatrist who rejects the existence of God and the supernatural?

3. What would be the difference in advice between a psychologist who believes in the reality of sin and guilt because God establishes what is right and wrong and one who believes that society decides what is right and wrong?

4. How would you answer someone who says that he resents blacks because they seem to be the ones who mug people on public transportation, in parks, and on the streets of large cities?

5. Should a church in a racially mixed neighborhood have a representation of those races in its congregation to consider itself unprejudiced?

6. Critique the following evangelistic invitation: "Put your trust in Jesus Christ, and He will bring fulfillment to your life."

7. Critique the following statement made during an evangelistic message: "Repent of sin, and realize you are rebellious and absolutely worthless!"

NOTES FOR CHAPTER 6

1. Kurt W. Fisher, contributor, *Psychology Today: An Introduction*, 2d ed. (New York: CRM/Random House, 1975), p. 19.

2. Sigmund Freud, *Totem and Taboo*, vol. 13 of *The Standard Edition of the Complete Psychological Works of Sigmund Freud*, trans. James Strachey (London: Hogarth, 1955), pp. 18, 67, 159.

3. B. F. Skinner, *Beyond Freedom and Dignity* (New York: Alfred A. Knopf, 1971), p. 74.

4. O. Hobart Mowrer, *The Crisis in Psychiatry and Religion* (New York: D. Van Nostrand, 1961).

5. Karl Menninger, *Whatever Became of Sin?* (New York: Hawthorn, 1973).

6. Mowrer, *The Crisis in Psychiatry and Religion*, p. 54.

7. Millard Erickson, *Christian Theology* (Grand Rapids: Baker, 1986), p. 642.

SELECT BIBLIOGRAPHY

Anderson, Ray S. *On Being Human*. Grand Rapids: Eerdmans, 1982.

Babbage, Stuart B. *Man in Nature and Grace*. Grand Rapids: Eerdmans, 1957.

Barth, Karl. *Church Dogmatics*. Edinburgh: T. and T. Clark, 1956-60. III/1, 2; IV/1, 2.

Berkouwer, G. C. *Man: The Image of God*. Grand Rapids: Eerdmans, 1962.

Bromiley, Geoffrey W. "Image of God." In *International Standard Bible Encyclopedia*. Rev. ed., 2:803-5. Grand Rapids: Eerdmans, 1979-88.

Brunner, Emil. *Man in Revolt*. Philadelphia: Westminster, 1947.

Carey, George. *I Believe in Man*. Grand Rapids: Eerdmans, 1977.

Calvin, John. *Institutes of the Christian Religion*. 2 vol. Edited by John T. McNeill and translated by Ford Lewis Battles. Philadelphia: Westminster, 1960.

Cosgrove, Mark P. *The Essence of Human Nature*. Grand Rapids: Zondervan, 1977.

Custance, Arthur C. *Man in Adam and Christ*. Grand Rapids: Zondervan, 1975.

De Graaff, Arnold, and James Olthuis, eds. *Toward a Biblical View of Man.* Toronto: Institute for Christian Studies, 1978.

Delitzsch, Franz. *A System of Biblical Psychology.* 2d ed. Translated by Robert Wallis. Edinburgh: T. and T. Clark, 1867.

Demarest, Bruce A. "Fall of Man." In *Evangelical Dictionary of Theology.* Grand Rapids: Baker, 1984.

Eichrodt, Walther. *Man in the Old Testament.* Translated by K. and R. Gregor Smith. London: SCM, 1954.

Erickson, Millard. *Christian Theology,* pp. 473-658. Grand Rapids: Baker, 1986.

Gundry, Robert H. *Soma in Biblical Theology: With Emphasis on Pauline Anthropology.* Cambridge, England: Cambridge U., 1975.

Harris, R. Laird. *Man—God's Eternal Creation: Old Testament Teaching on Man and His Culture.* Chicago: Moody, 1971.

Henry, Carl F. H. "Image of God." In *Evangelical Dictionary of Theology.* Grand Rapids: Baker, 1984.

Hocking, David L. *Who Am I and What Difference Does It Make?* Portland, Oreg.: Multnomah, 1985.

Hoekema, Anthony A. *Created in God's Image.* Grand Rapids: Eerdmans, 1988.

Jewett, Paul K. *Man as Male and Female.* Grand Rapids: Eerdmans, 1975.

Kummel, Werner G. *Man in the New Testament.* Translated by John J. Vincent. Revised and enlarged ed. London: Epworth, 1963.

Laidlaw, John. *The Bible Doctrine of Man.* Edinburgh: T. and T. Clark, 1895.

Machen, J. Gresham. *The Christian View of Man.* New York: Macmillan, 1937.

McDonald, H. D. *The Christian View of Man.* Westchester, Ill.: Crossway, 1981.

MacLeod, Donald. "Paul's Use of the Term 'The Old Man.'" *The Banner of Truth* 92 (May 1971): 13-19.

Moltmann, Jurgen. *Man: Christian Anthropology in the Conflicts of the Present.* Translated by John Sturdy. Philadelphia: Fortress, 1974.

Niebuhr, Reinhold. *The Nature and Destiny of Man: A Christian Interpretation.* New York: Scribner, 1941.

Orr, James. *God's Image in Man.* Grand Rapids: Eerdmans, 1948.

Packer, J. I. *Knowing Man.* Westchester, Ill.: Cornerstone, 1978.

Pannenberg, Wolfhart. *Human Nature, Election and History.* Philadelphia: Westminster, 1977.

Robinson, H. Wheeler. *The Christian Doctrine of Man.* Edinburgh: T. and T. Clark, 1911.

Ryrie, Charles C. "Total Depravity." In *Evangelical Dictionary of Theology.* Grand Rapids: Baker, 1984.

Stacey, W. D. *The Pauline View of Man.* London: Macmillan, 1956.

Stam, Cornelius R. *Man: His Nature and Destiny.* Chicago: Berean Bible Society, 1961.

Torrance, T. F. *Calvin's Doctrine of Man.* London: Lutterworth, 1949.

Van Peursen, C. A. *Body, Soul, Spirit: A Survey of the Body-Mind Problem.* Translated by H. H. Hoskins. London: Oxford, 1966.

Verduin, Leonard. *Somewhat Less Than God: The Biblical View of Man.* Grand Rapids: Eerdmans, 1970.

Wolff, Walter. *Anthropology of the Old Testament.* Philadelphia: Fortress, 1974.

GENERAL INDEX

SCRIPTURE INDEX